The Economics of Divorce: The Effects on Parents and Children

The Economics of Divorce: The Effects on Parents and Children

Craig A. Everett, PhD
Editor

Routledge
Taylor & Francis Group
NEW YORK AND LONDON

First published 1994 by
The Haworth Press, Inc., 10 Alice Street, Binghamton, NY 13904-1580, USA

Published 2016 by Routledge
Taylor and Francis Group
711 Third Avenue,
New York, NY 10017, USA

Routledge
Taylor and Francis Group
2 Park Square,
Milton Park, Abingdon,
Oxfordshire OX14 4RN

First issued in paperback 2016

Routledge is an imprint of the Taylor and Francis Group, an informa business

The Economics of Divorce: The Effects on Parents and Children **has been published as** ***Journal of Divorce & Remarriage,*** **Volume 22, Numbers 1/2 1994.**

Library of Congress Cataloging-in-Publication Data

The economics of divorce : the effects on parents and children / Craig A. Everett, editor.
p. cm.
"The economics of divorce: the effects on parents and children" has been published as Journal of divorce & remarriage, volume 22, numbers 1/2 1994"–CIP t.p. verso.
Includes bibliographical references.
ISBN 1-56024-694-4 (alk. paper)
1. Divorce–Economic aspects. 2. Divorced parents–Economic conditions. 3. Children of divorced parents–Economic conditions. I. Craig A. Everett.
HQ814.E26 1994
306.89–dc20

94-28287
CIP

ISBN 13: 978-1-138-98911-5 (pbk)
ISBN 13: 978-1-56024-694-7 (hbk)

The Economics of Divorce: The Effects on Parents and Children

CONTENTS

ABOUT THE EDITOR

Craig A. Everett, PhD, is a marriage and family therapist in private practice in Tucson, Arizona, and Director of the Arizona Institute of Family Therapy. In addition to his 20 years of experience in clinical practice, he was formerly President of the American Association for Marriage and Family Therapy. Dr. Everett's previous positions include Director of Family Therapy Training and Associate Professor at both Florida State University and Auburn University. He has been the Editor of the *Journal of Divorce & Remarriage* (formerly the *Journal of Divorce*) since 1983 and is an editorial board member of six professional journals.

Introduction

Everyone who works with divorcing families–whether they are clinicians, educators, mediators or attorneys–recognizes the critical role that economic factors play throughout the divorce process. We have all seen the outcome of divorce cases determined by which parent (or their families of origin) could pay for the "best" attorney. We have seen non-custodial parents who were angry over what they believed to be excessive financial obligations either withdraw from their children or continue the adversarial fight for years after the divorce. We have seen the custody of children bargained away for more favorable considerations in property settlements or reduced spousal maintenance awards. And we know that two post-divorce families "cannot live as cheaply as one."

In 1991, after over a year of collecting relevant manuscripts, I edited a special volume entitled "The Consequences of Divorce: Economic and Custodial Impact on Children and Adults." Even though the available manuscripts were very general in their treatment of economic factors, I believed that these issues were crucial enough to begin to formally identify them. Now, five years later, I am delighted to edit this special collection with ten articles focused entirely on the economic factors of divorce.

The research is now able to focus on more specific variables that will be relevant to the entire field. Such issues as the role of work and employment as well as the influence of intergenerational financial support are identified here. Other articles deal with the children's financial support for college and the economics of remarried

[Haworth co-indexing entry note]: "Introduction." Everett, Craig A. Co-published simultaneously in *Journal of Divorce & Remarriage* (The Haworth Press, Inc.) Vol. 22, No. 1/2, 1994, pp. 1-2; and: *The Economics of Divorce: The Effects on Parents and Children* (ed: Craig A. Everett) The Haworth Press, Inc., 1994, pp. 1-2. Multiple copies of this article/chapter may be purchased from The Haworth Document Delivery Center [1-800-3-HAWORTH; 9:00 a.m. - 5:00 p.m. (EST)].

families. I hope this collection of works will stimulate further research in this area.

Craig A. Everett, PhD
Tucson, AZ

Work or Marriage? Competence in Custodial Mothers in the Stabilization Phase of the Divorce Process

Solly Dreman
Roy Aldor

SUMMARY. Sense of competence, time perspective, and state-anxiety of custodial mothers in the "stabilization phase" of the divorce process were examined. These mothers had a more integrative general and parental sense of competence as well as lower levels of state-anxiety as compared to mothers located in the earlier phases of divorce, as predicted by a developmental model of divorce. Mothers in this phase who denied and overrated parental competence, however, had children who displayed poorer adjustment. While mothers had an integrative sense of competence on sex-stereotyped roles considered appropriate, such as housekeeper, they had a less integrative sense of competence on out-of-role tasks like provider, with domestic and occupational roles found to be incompatible. Similarly,

Solly Dreman, PhD, is Associate Professor and Director, and Roy Aldor, PhD, is Research Coordinator, Center for Family Life Research and Counseling, Ben Gurion University of the Negev, Beer Sheva, 84105, Israel.

The authors gratefully acknowledge the assistance of the National Insurance Institute for their help in identifying custodial mothers participating in this research.

All correspondence should be sent to Solly Dreman, PhD, Department of Behavioral Sciences, Ben Gurion University of the Negev, Beer Sheva, 84105, Israel.

[Haworth co-indexing entry note]: "Work or Marriage? Competence in Custodial Mothers in the Stabilization Phase of the Divorce Process." Dreman, Solly, and Roy Aldor. Co-published simultaneously in *Journal of Divorce & Remarriage* (The Haworth Press, Inc.) Vol. 22, No. 1/2, 1994, pp. 3-22; and: *The Economics of Divorce: The Effects on Parents and Children* (ed: Craig A. Everett) The Haworth Press, Inc., 1994, pp. 3-22. Multiple copies of this article/chapter may be purchased from The Haworth Document Delivery Center [1-800-3-HAWORTH; 9:00 a.m. - 5:00 p.m. (EST)].

mothers who increased their employment level postdivorce valued remarriage less. In contrast to the divorce model presented, mothers' time perspective was found to be discontinuous, the past being rated significantly more negatively than the present and future. Divorced mothers also displayed high levels of state-anger which correlated negatively with their ratings of the past, these ratings being related to poor adjustment in children. Treatment and research implications were discussed.

Single-parenthood may force divorced women to assume exclusive responsibility for themselves and their children and produce an enhanced sense of competence (Mitchell, 1983). Sense of competence in custodial mothers is important since it has been shown to be related to the postdivorce adjustment of children (Kanoy, Cunningham, White, & Adams, 1985; Pett, 1982; Wallerstein & Kelly, 1980).

Dreman, Orr, and Aldor (1989, 1990) studied sense of competence in divorced mothers using a developmental model of divorce (Herz Brown, 1988) to generate hypotheses about coping and adjustment. According to this model, mothers in the initial "aftermath" phase of divorce experience reactions of shock and bewilderment similar to those occurring in people struck by a natural disaster like an earthquake. This phase, which lasts about a year, is characterized by high anxiety and poor reality testing. It is followed by a transitional period called the "realignment" phase, in which parents try to understand their mistakes in the former marriage and undergo an "emotional divorce" from their former spouse and family. This phase lasts two to three years and is characterized by improved reality testing. In the final "stabilization" phase, occurring about four years from divorce, earlier cognitive and emotional resolution contributes to a new integrative sense of competence and solid identity in both familial and extrafamilial roles.

Dreman et al. (1989, 1990) studied sense of competence in groups of divorced women located in the aftermath phase (median separation time 4 mos.) and in the realignment phase (median separation time 22 mos.). *Sense of competence* was defined as "feeling in control of both general and specific life areas." Its components are *self-esteem*, reflecting subjective feelings of self-worth, prone to cognitive-emotional distortion, and *self-efficacy*, representing more objective action potential (Dreman, Orr, & Aldor, 1989). An *integrative sense of competence* is evidenced by positive congruent ratings of self-esteem and self-efficacy. These investigators hypothesized that women in the aftermath phase, experiencing high anxiety, shock, and bewilderment, would engage in defensive denial expressed in inflated ratings of parental self-esteem designed to protect the self, rather than coping with new realities such as diminished parental efficacy and high state-anxiety. Women in the realignment phase, emerging from the initial trauma, should display lower levels of anxiety and more realistic ratings of self-esteem which more accurately depict parental efficacy.

Dreman et al. (1989, 1990) found that low efficacy characterized women in both the aftermath and realignment phases, supporting research that shows that the first two years postdivorce are marked by decreased parental efficacy (Hetherington, Stanley-Hagan, & Anderson, 1989; Wallerstein & Kelly, 1980). As predicted, women in the aftermath had higher state-anxiety scores as well as significantly higher ratings of self-esteem than efficacy, while women in realignment had lower state-anxiety scores as well as lower self-esteem scores which more realistically reflected their low efficacy levels. These investigators concluded that the high self-esteem ratings of women in aftermath reflected defensive denial in the face of high state anxiety and low efficacy, while women in the realignment phase had emerged from the aftermath crisis, as evidenced in lower state-anxiety and more congruent self-esteem and efficacy ratings, indicating better reality testing. Women in realignment also had a more continuous and positive time perspective–an indication of more positive self-evaluation (Erikson, 1950).

The present study is an extension of these earlier studies and investigates sense of competence in divorced women located in the stabilization phase of the divorce process, median separation time 7 years. In accordance with Herz Brown's model, it was predicted that custodial mothers in this phase would display a positive integrative sense of general and parental competence, a continuous time perspective, and normal levels of state-anxiety. Sense of competence and time perspective were measured by employing the Competence Concepts and Time Perspective Semantic Differential Test (Dreman & Orr, 1985), while parental state-anxiety was measured by using the State-Trait Anxiety Inventory (Spielberger, Gorsuch, & Lushene, 1970).

The present study is unique in that in contrast to previous studies which only assessed *parental coping* (Dreman et al., 1989, 1990), it investigates the relationship between parental coping mechanisms like denial and *children's adjustment*. While most mothers were expected to have an integrated sense of general and parental competence in the stabilization phase, it was predicted that mothers who were "deniers," i.e., mothers with higher parental self-esteem than efficacy scores and high levels of state-anxiety, would have more maladjusted children. This follows since these mothers do not accurately assess their parental efficacy and are more likely to neglect children's postdivorce needs. Children's adjustment was assessed employing the General Self-Worth Scale of the Perceived Competence Scale (Harter, 1982) and the State-Anxiety Scale of the State-Trait Anxiety Inventory for Children (Spielberger, Edwards, Lushene, Montuori, & Platzak, 1973).

In addition to assessing general and parental competence, the divorced mothers' sense of competence and attitudes in such domains as occupational vs. domestic roles and single-parent vs. married parent status is investigated. Some researchers have concluded that marriage in the 20th century produces profound discontinuities in the lives of women, affecting their psychological and physical health (Bernard, 1982; Carter & McGoldrick, 1988; Hochschild, 1989). Marriage often hinders contemporary women in their career and other pursuits, while leaving them feeling alone in domestic roles like child care and housekeeping. However, while divorce may result in an increased sense of competence and independence in these women, since they have to take on new responsibilities (Mitchell, 1983), it may also exacerbate the conflict between domestic and occupational demands since many women increase their work load after divorce while still having to maintain the same level of domestic duties (Hartman, 1991; Hetherington, Stanley-Hagan, & Anderson, 1989). Such postdivorce developments could result in considerable ambivalence regarding married vs. single-parent status and domestic vs. occupational roles. The present study intends to investigate sense of competence and attitudes to these conflicting roles by having these mothers assess such concepts as "housekeeper," "provider," "married mother," "remarriage" and "mother alone" on the semantic differential instrument described earlier. This instrument measures, in addition to general and parental competence, a wide array of competence and attitudinal domains portraying the divorced parent.

Divorced women experience feelings of work overload, financial hardship, and loneliness after divorce (Katz, 1991). Relatedly, research shows that divorced women are characterized by unresolved feelings of anger associated with their divorce, as well as attribution of blame to the ex-spouse for the marital failure, even several years past divorce (Kitson & Sussman, 1982; Wallerstein, 1986). The present study attempts to investigate such processes in divorced women located in the stabilization phase, with parental anger measured by employing the State-Anger Scale of the State-Trait Anger Expression Inventory (STAXI) (Spielberger, 1988).

METHOD

Subjects

The sample consisted of 88 divorced custodial mothers who had obtained full custody of all their children, with at least one child between the ages 6 to 17 years of age. None of the divorced women in our sample had remarried. The ethnic composition of these mothers was 55% born in Israel, 20% of Asian-African origins and 25% born in western countries. Educational levels consisted of 5% with a masters degree or higher, 36% with some university education, 57% with high school education, and 2% with no formal education. The mean separation time was 8 years, median 7 years, and range 4-19 years. The mean number of years married was 10.5 years, median = 9 years, and range 1-38 years. The mean age of the mothers was 40 years, range 26-58 years. The mean age of the children examined was 14 years, median 15 years, and the range 5-19 years.

Measures

The Competence Concepts and Time Perspective Semantic Differential Test (Dreman & Orr, 1985). Sense of competence and time perspective were measured by a semantic differential instrument, employed in research with separated, divorced and married parents in Israel (Dreman et al., 1989, 1990). In the present study sense of competence was assessed by two *personal concepts*, Myself and Myself Mother which measure general and parental competence, two *role concepts*, Provider and Housekeeper related to sex-stereotyped roles, and three *marital status concepts*, Mother Alone, Married Mother, and Remarriage which were considered as reflecting how much a divorced parent values single- vs. married-parent status.

The seven competence concepts, as well as three time perspective concepts, Past, Present, and Future, were rated on several semantic differential scales. These scales were divided into four *evaluative* scales (good-bad, pleasant-unpleasant, fair-unfair, beautiful-ugly), and three *activity* scales (active-passive, fast-slow, sharp-dull). They are derived from the major factors, with their bipolar adjectives, of the Semantic Differential Rating Scale (Osgood, Suci, & Tannenbaum, 1955). The concepts were presented in different sequences and within concept polar adjectives were reversed to control for order effects. Adjectives were rated on a 7-point scale and were coded so that a score of 7 indicated a high score on any factor. *Self-esteem* is represented by the evaluative factor of the semantic differential, which corresponds to the emotional and cognitive valence component of attitudes (Krech, Crutchfield, & Ballachey, 1962). *Self-efficacy* is represented by the activity factor of the semantic differential which represents an "oriented activity factor" (Weinrich, 1969) measuring action potential. This test has been extensively tested in previous divorce research, and measures of internal reliability and validity have been demonstrated (for a more detailed description see Dreman et al., 1989).

The State-Trait Anxiety Scale (Spielberger, Gorsuch, & Lushene, 1970). This self-report test obtained measures of subject's situational or state-anxiety. The scale includes 20 anxiety-related items, rated on a 4 point scale, ranging from "not at all" to "very much so." This instrument is well known for its high validity and reliability, and the Hebrew version used (Teichman & Melink, 1978) has been tested previously in divorce-related research in Israel (Dreman et al., 1989, 1990).

State-Trait Anger Expression Inventory (STAXI) (Spielberger, 1988). The STAXI consists of 44 self-report items, rated on a four-point scale, which form six scales: State-Anger, Trait-Anger, Anger-in, Anger-out, Anger-Control and Anger-Expression. This inventory was used in an analysis of custodial parents' anger postdivorce. Specifically, we used the 10-item state-anger scale translated to Hebrew by the authors which had an alpha of .92. This scale measures the intensity of anger feelings at a particular time on a 4-point scale ranging from "not at all" to "very much so." For a complete description of this instrument, including measures of reliability and validity, see Spielberger (1988).

The State-Trait Anxiety Inventory for Children (Spielberger, Edwards, Lushene, Montuori, & Platzak, 1973). The state-anxiety scale, which measures situational anxiety, was used as a measure of children's postdivorce adjustment. This scale contains 20 items with a 3-point scale measuring the presence or absence of each anxiety item, e.g., "very anxious," "anxious," and "not anxious." A Hebrew version of this scale with proven reliability and validity was used (Teichman & Melink, 1979). The alpha obtained for the present administration of the scale was .86.

The Perceived Competence Scale for Children (Harter, 1982). A shortened 3-item version of the General Self-Worth Scale was used which had been translated to Hebrew by the authors. The internal reliability of this scale was .73 and is comparable to the alpha cited for the whole 7-item scale (Harter, 1982). The items were rated on a 3-point scale ranging from "not so true," "sort of true," to "very true."

Procedure

The custodial mothers are a subsample of parents participating in a large longitudinal research project investigating coping and adjustment in divorced custodial families. Parents were located through the assistance of the National Insurance Institute which has updated lists of divorced custodial parents who receive regular child stipends from the Institute. Parents were approached by mail under Institute letterhead and asked if they were willing to participate in a research project studying single-parent families. Those who agreed were asked to sign a waver of confidentiality. The response rates were 18.5% for mothers which were considered adequate in the Israeli context (Hornik & Meir, 1989). The parents who replied were subsequently mailed a structured questionnaire including various measures of coping and adjustment. After the questionnaire was returned, home visits were scheduled in which the parent underwent further testing. At that time a target child, between the ages of 6 and 17 years, was also interviewed on measures of coping and adjustment. Testing in the home setting was done by upper level psychology students who were specially trained and supervised for this task. Anonymity was insured and parents were told that they would receive general information regarding the study at a later date. Group meetings were held with parents in order to help them deal with some of the normative difficulties of divorce.

RESULTS

For purpose of analysis, sense of competence is considered *integrative* when a given concept is rated positively, with the self-esteem and efficacy factors congruent. Sense of competence is considered as defensive, indicating *denial*, when self-esteem is rated high, though efficacy levels are low. Another criterion for defensive denial will be when self-esteem scores are of high magnitude, even though state anxiety ratings are high. This follows since high self-esteem in the face of high state-anxiety may be indicative of protecting sense of competence in the face of threat. When self-esteem is less than efficacy, this will be considered as indicative of *underestimating* one's competence in any given area.

Competence Concepts

A 7 × 2 (competence concepts × factor scores) MANOVA revealed a significant interaction effect ($F(6,522) = 35.28$, $p < .001$ (see Table 1 for means and results of MANOVA).

On the *personal competence concepts*, Myself and Myself Mother, a 2 × 2 MANOVA revealed a marginally significant factor score main effect $F(1,87) = 3.90$, $p < .052$), with self-esteem being slightly higher than efficacy on these concepts. However, the mag-

TABLE 1. Mean competence concepts and time perspective items Semantic differential factor scores.

Concept	E	A
Myself	5.85	5.68
Myself Mother	6.18	5.94
Provider	4.34	5.33
Housekeeper	5.24	5.28
Mother Alone	4.00	5.34
Married Mother	6.05	5.50
Remarriage	5.45	4.71
Future	5.69	5.40
Present	5.41	5.42
Past	3.38	4.58

Key: E = evaluative factor A = activity factor
Competence concepts SDs ranged from 0.82 to 1.76.
Time perspective SDs ranged from 1.34 to 1.90.

nitude of the factor scores within each concept suggests that both general and parental sense of competence are positive and integrative.

Parental competence, denial, and children's adjustment. Custodial mothers were divided into three subgroups reflecting degree of congruence on the parental competence item, Myself Mother: "deniers"–those whose self-esteem exceeded their self-efficacy scores by more than half a standard deviation (SD = 0.94); "congruent"–those whose self-esteem and efficacy scores were not more than half a standard deviation apart and "underestimators"–those whose self-esteem scores were more than half a standard deviation below their self-efficacy scores. Altogether, 53% of the mothers were congruent, while 17% and 30% were under- or over-estimators. Corroborating evidence of the defensiveness of those mothers labelled "deniers" was the finding that they had higher state-anxiety than the congruent mothers (M's = 2.30 vs. 1.98, $F(1,85) = 4.29$, $p < .041$). Two child self-report adjustment measures, state-anxiety and self-worth, were included in a one-way (degree of congruence) MANOVA. A significant main effect was obtained for degree of congruence across both measures ($F(4,166) = 2.57$, $p < .04$). Inspection of Table 2 reveals that congruent mothers had children who rated themselves highest on self-worth and rated their state-anxiety lower than children whose mothers were deniers. Children of mothers who denied reported the highest levels of state-anxiety and relatively low levels of self-worth compared to the congruent mothers. Hence, defensive denial by divorced mothers, in the stabilization phase, was associated with relatively poor adjustment in children as measured by their own self-reports.

On *role competence concepts*, a 2 × 2 MANOVA revealed a highly significant interaction effect ($F,(1,87) = 21.30$, $p < .001$). Custodial mothers were positive and congruent on the Housekeeper role, but had significantly lower ratings on self-esteem than efficacy on the Provider role ($F,(1,87) = 28.98$, $p < .001$). On the basis of this low appraisal of Provider, it was hypothesized that work and domestic roles may be incompatible for these women. In support of this contention were the zero-order correlations obtained between the Housekeeper and Provider roles on both the self-esteem and self-efficacy factors.

TABLE 2. Mean children's self-report adjustment scores as a function of custodial mother's degree of congruence on parental sense of competence.

	Children's adjustment	
Mothers' congruence	State-anxiety	Self-worth
Congruent	1.45	2.70
Over-estimators	1.53	2.37
Under-estimators	1.44	2.33

State-anxiety SDs ranged from 0.18 to 0.31.
Self-worth SDs ranged from 0.42 to 0.71.

On roles depicting *marital status*, a 3 × 2 MANOVA revealed a highly significant interaction effect (F,(2,174) = 61.39, p < .001). Mothers rated Married Mother and Remarriage highly as compared to Mother Alone which they rated quite low on the self-esteem factor (F(1,87) = 13.19, p < .001). Similarly, these mothers displayed ambivalence to their single-parent status as evidenced by their significantly lower self-esteem as compared to self-efficacy scores on Mother Alone (F(1,87 = 46.42, p < .001). However, they also appear ambivalent towards remarriage as evidenced by the fact that in spite of their positive self-esteem score on this concept, their efficacy, i.e, action potential towards remarriage is significantly lower (F(1,87) = 34.45, p < .001).

Employment status and remarriage. We previously suggested that domestic and occupational tasks were not compatible, as indicated by the zero-order correlations obtained between the Housekeeper and Provider concepts. In view of this finding we hypothesized that women who become more self-sufficient occupationally after divorce may be less willing to remarry and return to traditional domestic roles. A posthoc examination of the effect of changes in employment level on Remarriage was done to examine this hypothesis. Divorced women were divided into 3 subgroups according to their employment level after divorce: increased employment (26%), status quo (55%), and decreased employment (19%). Education and anxiety levels were treated as covariates of employment levels, since previous research in Israel has found that increased education/SES positively correlates with being divorced (Peres & Katz, 1981), while increased state-anxiety is associated with a diminished inclination for divorcees to remarry (Dreman et al., 1990). In a 3 × 2 (work level × factor scores) MANCOVA, a significant main effect was obtained for employment, with women who had increased employment levels after divorce displaying lower ratings of Remarriage on the evaluative factor, as compared to women in the status quo or diminished employment groups (Remarriage means [increased employment, status quo, decreased employment] = 4.92, 5.49, 6.19, respectively (F(2,80) = 2.93, p < .05). From these findings it may be inferred that mothers who increase their employment levels after divorce are less willing to remarry than are those who have decreased or maintained the same occupational status, even when educational and state-anxiety levels are controlled.

Time Perspective Concepts

A 3 × 2 MANOVA (time perspective × factor scores) revealed a significant main effect for time perspective ($F(2,174) = 49.36, p < .001$), with the Past rated as significantly more negative than the Present or Future (see Table 1). A significant time × factor score interaction was obtained ($F(2, 174) = 29.03, p < .001$) and a further analysis revealed that while mothers rated the Present and Future positively and congruently, the Past was rated negatively on the evaluative factor and significantly lower than the activity factor ($F(1,87) = 33.13, p < .001$). Inspection of Table 1 reveals that the Past was rated more negatively on the evaluative factor than any other semantic differential item.

State-Anxiety

As predicted, these custodial mothers, located in the stabilization phase, had low levels of state-anxiety ($M = 2.06$). These levels were considerably lower than those of mothers tested in the aftermath and realignment phases (M's = 2.62 and 2.48, respectively) and comparable to those of a normative group of Israeli married mothers ($M = 2.08$) (Dreman, Orr, & Aldor, 1989, 1990). A negative correlation was obtained between state-anxiety and self-esteem across the seven competence concepts tested ($r = -.38, p < .01$). This is indicative of good reality testing by these divorced women since low state-anxiety is associated with high competence and high state-anxiety with low competence.

State-Trait Anger Expression Inventory

The divorced mothers' state-anger was found to be considerably higher than that reported by Spielberger (1988) for normative samples of American women (M's: Israeli divorced women (mean age 40) = 14.60; American women (age 31-40) = 12.61; American women (age 41 and older) = 10.82). The divorced mothers' state-anger was also higher than the mean state-anger scores obtained for a sample of first-year Israeli university women ($M = 12.17$),[1] even though state-anger has been reported to decrease with age (Spielberger, 1988).

Anger, attributions, and children's adjustment. Since ratings of state-anger and attributions towards the past were highly negative, a posthoc analysis was undertaken inspecting the relation between these negative affective and attributional parental states on children's adjustment as measured by the self-worth and state-anxiety scales. The divorced mothers' state-anger was negatively correlated with their ratings of the past on the evaluative factor ($r = -.21$ $p <$ .04), with more negative ratings of the past being related to poorer adjustment in children on both self-worth (r(past. self-worth) = +.19. $p < .06$) and state-anxiety (r (past. state-anxiety) = – .26, $p <$ .02). These findings suggest that mothers' state-anger not only adversely affects their ratings of the past, but these negative attributions in turn adversely affect children's adjustment.

DISCUSSION

Custodial mothers in the present study had an integrative sense of general and parental competence. The positive congruent ratings of these mothers, as compared to the less congruent and less positive sense of competence found in subjects at earlier stages (Dreman et al., 1989, 1990), support Herz Brown's (1988) model of a developmental progression, as divorced parents move from the aftermath and realignment to the stabilization phase of divorce. These mothers, as a whole, had normal levels of state-anxiety, which may in part explain their diminished defensiveness, good reality testing, and integrative sense of competence. Noteworthy was the finding that mothers who denied, i.e, had higher ratings of parental self-esteem than efficacy and had higher levels of state-anger, had children who reported poorer adjustment than children of mothers with congruent ratings of parental competence. Hence, defensive parental coping strategies, such as denial, may adversely affect children's adjustment in the stabilization phase of the divorce process.

A recent review of gender differences in divorce concluded that women display better postdivorce adjustment than men (Diedrick,

1991). Similarly, they attain new levels of personal and occupational competence as compared to men, with these differences persisting even ten years after the divorce event (Keith, 1985; Wallerstein, 1986). Diedrick (1991) suggests that this may be due to the fact that women assume traditionally masculine roles which are valued by society such as being a provider, while men may have to take on devalued feminine roles such as being a housekeeper postdivorce. For women, such role changes may result in an increased sense of esteem (Bardwick, 1911) and a diminished desire to remarry. Supporting the contention of occupationally related self-esteem was our finding that custodial mothers valued remarriage less the more their postdivorce employment levels increased, even when educational and state anxiety levels were partialled. Further evidence of the importance of occupational pursuits for women is a study in Israel which found that postdivorce occupational growth was a major factor contributing to the well-being of divorced mothers, located an average of eight years past divorce (Katz, 1991).

While women who become more self-sufficient as providers may experience increased self-esteem postdivorce, they may also encounter adverse gender-linked attitudes which reduce esteem attached to such "out-of-role" behaviors. Supporting this hypothesis was our finding that while custodial mothers had positive congruent attitudes towards being a housekeeper and married mother, they had lower self-esteem on the provider and mother alone roles, despite their high efficacy in these roles. Israel promotes "familism," where high positive valence is attached to marriage and family, children occupying a central position in family life (Peres & Katz, 1991; Shamgar-Handelman & Bar-Yosef, 1991). Sex-role stereotypes are traditional (Dreman, 1978, 1982; Katz & Pesach, 1985), with men being the main wage earners, women devoting their main psychological and physical efforts to children and family (Bar-Yosef, 1969; Peres & Katz, 1981). Only 3% of the population has remained single till age 50 in Israel (Population and Housing Census, 1983) and maintaining stability of the family is a socially recognized goal (Friedlander & Goldsheider, 1979). Lower self-esteem in the face of high efficacy on the mother alone and provider roles may therefore reflect the low value Israeli society attaches to deviance from traditional roles of married mother and housekeeper.

In the present study, we found that the housekeeper and provider roles were not correlated in the custodial mothers, while a related study found a positive correlation between these tasks in custodial fathers (Dreman & Aldo, in press). Research shows that working mothers maintain the same domestic responsibilities as nonworking mothers, resulting in a double work load (Hartman, 1991). This situation is particularly acute for divorced mothers who often increase their work load postdivorce, despite continuing and often increasing domestic demands (Hetherington, Stanley-Hagan, & Anderson, 1989). Custodial fathers, in contrast, can continue their career without undue difficulty, since many domestic tasks are taken over by female relatives (Greif, 1987). This may explain why the housekeeper and occupational roles were found to be less compatible for mothers than fathers.

The ambivalence regarding occupational vs. domestic roles for women was evidenced in a recent finding that while divorced women in Israel did perceive positive postdivorce changes in such life domains as professional development and self-confidence, they also perceived negative changes like increased loneliness, the lowering of material standards, and work overload (Katz, 1991). These women also had a lower sense of well-being as compared to a comparison group of married mothers. These findings, together with the earlier observations regarding familism, further explain why the Israeli divorcees value married motherhood highly as compared to single-parenthood.

Custodial mothers of the present study had high state-anger and rated the past very negatively, even though their median separation time was seven years. This finding confirms other divorce research which shows that divorced women express more anger, disappointment and dissatisfaction than do men and blame their ex-spouse for the divorce even several years past the divorce event (Kitson & Sussman, 1982; Wallerstein, 1986). Recent research on anger has shown that such affect may negatively influence cognitive processes such as memories and attributions, as well as action tendencies (Berkowitz, 1990; Dix, Reinhold, & Zambarno, 1990). Dix et al. (1990), for example, found that angry mothers judge children more negatively than mothers in a happy or neutral mood. These investigators proposed that anger with its negative affect may cause the parent to scan the environment for negative cues and attributions. While they suggested that such affect-related cognitive biases may ultimately adversely affect children's adjustment, they did not present any findings related to adjustment outcomes. The present study is unique in that it found that the mothers' anger was not only related to their *own* negative cognitive judgements, as expressed in their negative ratings of the past, but also adversely affected children's *self*-ratings of adjustment, when the past served as a mediating variable. Thus the pervasive anger and embitterment of divorced mothers may result in negative cognitive appraisals and/or attributions which adversely affect children's adjustment.

IMPLICATIONS AND CONCLUSIONS

The present study indicates that while divorced women may welcome their increased autonomy, traditional attitudes expressing familism and the ongoing domestic responsibilities of the working mother may cause considerable ambivalence concerning career goals. There is urgent need to modify gender-linked attitudes towards the division of domestic and occupational tasks in contemporary society, to provide proper child care facilities, and to implement a more equal distribution of such tasks in the contemporary family (Hochschild, 1989). In accordance with such goals, educational and treatment programs designed to encourage more androgenous attitudes and behaviors would be helpful in creating a more integrative sense of competence for parents on sex-stereotyped roles like being a bread-winner or housekeeper. Making such tasks more "ego-syntonic" will reduce ambivalence and increase esteem and competence associated with these roles. This is particularly important for divorced parents since they are often required to take on such out-of-role tasks due to demand characteristics of the postdivorce situation. The stabilization phase may be ideal for direct therapeutic work with such parents since in this stage they have lower levels of state-anxiety, facilitating the cognitive and emotional resolution necessary for change (Dreman & Aldor, in press).

While the present research demonstrated that divorced mothers had high levels of general and parental competence, they also demonstrate considerable anger and negative attributions towards the past, even though they are located several years past divorce. These negative affective and cognitive processes in mothers were found to be related to poorer adjustment in children. Intervention should be designed to diminish these adverse processes which contribute to poor postdivorce adjustment. For example, emotional resolution which helps these mothers integrate the positive as well as negative aspects of the past should diminish anger and negative attributions such as blaming the ex-spouse, thus promoting parental cooperation. This is important since postdivorce parental cooperation has been found to be related to good adjustment in children (Camara & Resnick, 1988, 1989). Such emotional resolution may also promote more mature choices of life-mates, not based on reactive "first-order" mechanisms (Watzlawick, Weakland, & Fisch, 1974) such as "cut-off," where one looks for the polar opposite of the ex-spouse or "more-of-the same," where one chooses a mate very similar to the one they divorced. In addition, while most women displayed an integrative sense of competence and low state-anxiety in the stabilization phase, intervention attempts might be aimed at locating and helping those mothers who are deniers. Intervention in this instance should attempt to help these mothers to appraise their parental competence realistically since overestimation of parental efficacy was found to be related to poor adjustment in children.

One limitation of this study is its cross-sectional nature, requiring that inferences made with regard to the divorce *process* be treated with caution. We are presently retesting all subjects as part of a longitudinal study of the coping and adjustment in custodial families, using a married control group for comparison. Another important issue concerns the mechanisms by which negative parental affect influences children's adjustment. Dix et al. (1990) suggested that when negative affect is chronic and intense in parents, anger-induced cognitive biases may distort appraisals of children, thus promoting negative parent-child interaction. Future studies might systematically investigate how anger, acting through such mediating variables as cognitive appraisals and parent-child interaction, ultimately affects children's adjustment. Illustrative of such an approach is a study by McKline, Johnston, and Tschann (1991) which found that parental conflict most strongly affected children's postdivorce adjustment through its adverse effect on parent-child relationships. Finally, cross-cultural research in countries with different degrees of familism/traditionalism should investigate how roles such as provider and housekeeper are rated in different cultural contexts. Such research would be helpful in identifying culture-bound and/or sexist attitudes which hinder adjustment in the postdivorce family.

NOTE

1. This figure was taken from the Hebrew validation and standardization of the STAXI being conducted by the present authors.

REFERENCES

Bar-Yosef, R. (1969). Role differentiation in Israeli urban families. In R. Bar-Yosef & I. Shelach (Eds.), *The family in Israel* (pp. 167-184). Jerusalem: Academon Press (in Hebrew).

Bardwick, J. (1971). *Psychology of women: A study of biocultural conflicts*. New York: Harper & Row.

Berkowitz, L. (1990). On the formation and regulation of anger and aggression: A cognitive-neoassociationistic analysis. *American Psychologist, 45*, 494-503.

Bernard, J. (1982). *The future of marriage*. New Haven, CT: Yale University Press.

Camara, K.A., & Resnick, G. (1988). Interparental conflict and cooperation: Factors moderating children's post-divorce adjustment. In E.M. Hetherington & J.D. Arasteh (Eds.), *Impact of divorce, single-parenting, and stepparenting on children* (pp. 169-195). Hillsdale, NJ: Erlbaum.

Camara, K.A., & Resnick, G. (1989). Styles of conflict resolution and cooperation between divorced parents: Effects on child behavior and adjustment. *American Journal of Orthopsychiatry, 59*, 560-575.

Carter, E.A., & McGoldrick, M. (1988). *The changing family life cycle: A framework of family therapy*. New York: Gardner Press.

Diedrick, P. (1991). Gender differences in divorce adjustment. *Journal of Divorce & Remarriage, 14*, 33-45.

Dix, T., Reinhold, D.P., & Zambarano, R.J. (1990). Mothers; judgements in moments of anger. *Merrill-Palmer Quarterly, 36*, 465-486.

Dreman, S. (1978). Sex-role stereotyping in mental health standards in Israel. *Journal of Clinical Psychology, 34*, 961-966.

Dreman, S. (1982). Sex role stereotyping and mental health standards in Israel: A cross-cultural comparison. in I. Gross, J. Downing, & A. d'Heurle (Eds.), *Sex role attitudes and cultural change.* Dordrecht, Holland, and Boston: D.R. Reidel Publishing Co.

Dreman, S., & Aldor, R. (in press). Competence and couplehood: A study of custodial mothers and fathers in the stabilization phase of the divorce process.

Dreman, S., & Orr, E. (1985). *Changes perceived by mothers occurring in the social, familial and personal constellation after filing for divorce in the rabbinical court in Israel.* Unpublished manuscript, Ben Gurion University of the Negev, Bandy Steiner Center for Single Parent Families, Beer Sheva.

Dreman, S., Orr, E., & Aldor, R. (1989). Competence of dissonance? Divorcing mothers' perceptions of sense of competence and time perspective. *Journal of Marriage and the Family, 52,* 405-415.

Dreman, S., Orr, E., & Aldor, R. (1990). Sense of competence, time perspective, and state-anxiety of separated vs. divorced mothers. *American Journal of Orthopsychiatry, 60,* 77-85.

Erikson, E.N. (1950). *Childhood and society.* New York: Norton.

Friedlander, D., & Goldsheider, C. (1979). *Populations of Israel.* New York: Columbia University Press.

Greif, G. (1987). A longitudinal examination of single custodial fathers: Implications for treatment. *The American Journal of Family Therapy, 15,* 253-260.

Harter, S. (1982). The perceived competence scale for children. *Child Development, 53,* 87-97.

Hartman, H. (1991). The division of labor in Israeli families. In L. Shamgar-Handleman & R. Bar-Yosef (Eds.), *Families in Israel.* Jerusalem: Academon–The Hebrew University. (in Hebrew).

Herz Brown, J. (1988). The postdivorce family. In B. Carter & M. McGoldrick (Eds.), *The changing family life cycle: A framework for family therapy* (pp. 371-398). New York: Gardner Press Inc.

Hetherington, E.M., Stanley-Hagan, M., & Anderson, E.R. (1989). Marital transitions: A child's perspective. *The American Psychologist, 44,* 303-312.

Hochschild, A. (1989). *Second shift: Working parents and the revolution at home.* New York: Viking.

Hornik, Y., & Meir, N. (1989). Meta-analysis of non-response in mail surveys. *Megamot, 32,* 386-400 (in Hebrew).

Kanoy, K.W., Cunningham, J.L., White, P., & Adams, J. (1984). Is family structure that critical? Family relationships of children with divorced and married parents. *Journal of Divorce, 8,* 97-105.

Katz, R., & Pesach, N. (1985). Adjustment to divorce in Israel: A comparison between divorced men and women. *Journal of Marriage and the Family, 47,* 765-772.

Katz, R. (1991). "Marital status and well-being" A comparison of widowed, divorced, and married women in Israel, *Journal of Divorce & Remarriage, 14,* 203-218.

Keith, P.M. (1985). Financial well-being of older divorced/separated men and women: Findings from a panel study. *Journal of Divorce, 9,* 61-72.

Kitson, G., & Sussman, M. (1982). Marital complaints, demographic characteristics, and symptoms of mental distress in divorce. *Journal of Marriage and the Family, 44*, 87-11.

Kline, M., Johnston, J.R., Tschann, J. (1991). The long shadow of marital conflict: A model of children's postdivorce adjustment. *Journal of Marriage and the Family, 53*, 297-309.

Krech, D., Crutchfield, R.S., & Ballachey, E.L. (1962). *Individual in society: A textbook of social psychology*. New York: McGraw Hill.

Mitchell, K.M. (1983). The price tag of responsibility: A comparison of divorced and remarried mothers. *Journal of Divorce, 5*, 33-42.

Osgood, C.E., Suci, G.J., & Tannenbaum, P.H. (1955). The principle of congruity in the prediction of attitude change. *Psychological Review, 62*, 42-55.

Peres, Y., & Katz, R. (1981). Stability and centrality: The nuclear family in modern Israel. *Social Forces, 59*, 687-704.

Peres, Y., & Katz, R. (1991).The family in Israel: Change and continuity. In L. Shamgar-Handleman & R. Bar-Yosef (Eds.), *Families in Israel*. Jerusalem: Academon–The Hebrew University (in Hebrew).

Pett, M.G. (1982). Correlates of children's social adjustment following divorce. *Journal of Divorce, 5*, 25-39.

Shamgar-Handleman, L., & Bar-Yosef, R. *Families in Israel*. Jerusalem: Academon–The Hebrew University of Jerusalem (in Hebrew).

Spielberger, C.D. (1988). *State-Trait Anger Expression Inventory*. Odessa, FL: Psychological Assessment Resources, Inc.

Spielberger, C.D., Edwards, C.D., Lushene, R.E., Montuori, J., & Platzek, D. (1973). *Preliminary Test Manual for the State-Trait Anxiety Inventory for Children*. Palo Alto, CA: Consulting Psychologists Press.

Spielberger, C.D., Gorsuch, R.L., & Lushene, R.E. (1970). *Manual for the State-Trait Anxiety Inventory*. Palo Alto, CA: Consulting Psychologists Press.

Teichman, Y., & Melink, C. (1979). *STAI, STAIC: Hebrew Manual*, Tel Aviv University: Ramot (in Hebrew).

Wallerstein, J.S. (1986). Women after divorce: Preliminary report from a ten-year follow-up. *American Journal of Orthopsychiatry, 56*, 65-77.

Wallerstein, J.S., & Kelly, J. (1980). *Surviving the breakup: How children and parents cope with the divorce*. New York: Basic Books.

Watzlawick, P., Weakland, J.H., & Fisch, R. (1974). *Change: Problems of problem formation and problem resolution*. New York: Norton.

Divorcees' Economic Well-Being and Financial Adequacy as Related to Interfamily Grants

Peggy S. Draughn
Ronda C. LeBoeuf
Patricia J. Wozniak
Frances C. Lawrence
Lisa R. Welch

SUMMARY. This study determined whether perceived financial adequacy, satisfaction with level of living, and perceived economic well-being following divorce were related to interfamily grants received by divorcees. Responses from 136 divorced individuals were analyzed using logistic regression, chi square analysis, and Spearman rank correlation.

Divorcees with physical custody of children and/or lower incomes perceived their finances to be inadequate more often than divorcees without children in the home and/or higher incomes. Perceived economic well-being was significantly related to the number of years divorced. Younger divorcees received more interfamily grants than older divorcees. Babysitting was the service most frequently received and most often, monthly. Clothes were more fre-

Peggy S. Draughn, PhD, is on the faculty, School of Human Ecology; Ronda C. LeBoeuf, MS, is a graduate student; Patricia J. Wozniak, PhD, is an Experimental Statistician; Frances C. Lawrence, PhD, is on the faculty, School of Human Ecology; Lisa R. Welch, MS, is a graduate student, School of Human Ecology. All are with the Louisiana Agricultural Experiment Station, Louisiana State University, Baton Rouge, LA 70803-4300.

[Haworth co-indexing entry note]: "Divorcees' Economic Well-Being and Financial Adequacy as Related to Interfamily Grants." Draughn, Peggy S. et al. Co-published simultaneously in *Journal of Divorce & Remarriage* (The Haworth Press, Inc.) Vol. 22, No. 1/2, 1994, pp. 23-35; and: *The Economics of Divorce: The Effects on Parents and Children* (ed: Craig A. Everett) The Haworth Press, Inc., 1994, pp. 23-35. Multiple copies of this article/chapter may be purchased from The Haworth Document Delivery Center [1-800-3-HAWORTH; 9:00 a.m. - 5:00 p.m. (EST)].

> quently received than any other type of goods. Individuals who scored higher on satisfaction with level of living received less assistance than those who scored lower on satisfaction with level of living. Females received significantly more goods and money than males received.

Married couples are considered an economic unit in Western society, and when divorce occurs, the spouses divide their assets and attempt to survive as two separate economic units (Bohannon, 1970). It is well-documented that women suffer more financially from this division than men (Adams & Adams, 1979; Albrecht, 1980; Albrecht, Bahr, & Goodman, 1983; Amato & Partridge, 1987; Bahr, 1983; Clark-Stewart & Bailey, 1989; Corcoran, 1979; Day & Bahr, 1986; Duncan & Hoffman, 1985; Espenshade, 1979; Halem, 1982; Hampton, 1975; Hoffman, 1977; Hoffman & Holmes, 1976; Mauldin, 1991; Rowe, 1989; Weiss, 1984; Weitzman, 1985), although men also may experience lowered financial adequacy. Various factors augment or diminish the negative effects of divorce on overall economic well-being. Earning power, child support, and child custody are the factors frequently cited in the literature (Duncan, 1984). Per capita income of women has been found to decrease substantially more than that of men after divorce (Day & Bahr, 1986). In 1990, over three million single mothers lived below the poverty threshold (U.S. Department of Commerce). In fact, the poverty rate among women is much higher after divorce, while men may experience improvement in economic well-being (Morgan, 1989). According to Bauer and Hogan (1987) individuals and families who believed their income was adequate managed their resources better than individuals and families who believed their income was inadequate. However, individuals and families who perceived their income to be adequate might have less money than families who believed their income to be inadequate. Others found divorcees' perceived economic well-being was not necessarily related to actual economic well-being (Halem, 1982; Keith, 1985). Subjective measures of economic well-being were found to be better indicators of family economic well-being than objective measures (Ackerman & Paolucci, 1983; Bauer & Hogan, 1987).

Very little research has been conducted in the area of practical assistance for divorcees. Practical assistance might alleviate some of the economic burden by reducing the services or goods purchased. In a classic study, Goode (1956) reported that divorced women usually obtained financial aid from their families, but no other types of assistance were reported. Men were not included in his study. Parents who disapproved of their child's divorce tended not to give support. In the 1980s, Gerstel (1988) and Johnson (1988) reported that both divorced men and women relied on family for practical assistance. However, none of these studies attempted to tie the receipt of practical assistance, i.e., interfamily grants, to economic well-being or financial adequacy.

Families, especially parents and siblings, contribute to offspring families in many ways. Strong, DeVault, Suid, and Reynolds (1983) described family contributions as money, interest-free loans, practical gifts, expenses involved in visits, and loans for down payments on a house. Both age of children and marital status of children were found to influence the likelihood of parental gifts. Married, older children were the least likely to receive help. Divorce status has not been adequately explored as a factor determining parental assistance.

There appears to be general consensus that a major problem experienced by divorcees is economic survival. We consider economic survival to be multifaceted. Financial adequacy, economic well-being, and satisfaction with level of living are components of economic survival. Perceived economic well-being is a subjective assessment by individuals as to their overall economic survival. Financial adequacy is a more objective term based on assessments of adequacy of income to meet financial demands for needs within a chosen lifestyle. Perceptions of ability to meet these needs without undue stress from concern over economic survival ability is reflected in satisfaction with level of living. Both monetary and practical assistance of goods and services may be provided by families for adult children. Whether divorcees receive interfamily grants to alleviate the economic burdens is not known. This study examines the types of assistance, if any, received from families and whether such interfamily grants are related to economic well-being, financial adequacy, and satisfaction with level of living.

METHODOLOGY

This study was a part of a larger project on adjustment following divorce. A 59-item questionnaire was developed to include three major problem areas often experienced by divorced individuals: child custody, reentry into social activities, and overall economic well-being. A fourth section identified types of assistance and asked how frequently such assistance was received. Demographic variables included were: age, payment or receipt of child support, education, and physical custody of children. This study focuses only on those items dealing with economic well-being, assistance and frequency of assistance, and the demographic variables.

Although individual items and services were listed and respondents checked each received and the frequency received, the following categories were formed for analysis: (1) *GOODS* (clothing, household necessities, food); (2) *SERVICES* (laundry, help with household chores, transportation, baby-sitting, chauffeuring to or from school or activities); and (3) *RECEIPT OF MONEY* (amount not specified). Frequency of assistance received was measured as *daily, weekly, monthly,* or *less than monthly.*

Operationalization of Terms

Overall economic well-being was measured by three components. *Financial adequacy* was assessed by the question: "Which of the following four statements describes your ability to get along on your income? (1) I can't make ends meet; (2) I have just enough, no more; (3) I have enough, with a little extra sometimes; and (4) I always have money left over" (Keith, 1985). *Satisfaction with level of living* was measured by the question: "Generally, how satisfied are you with how economically well-off you are now? (1) very unsatisfied; (2) unsatisfied; (3) satisfied; and (4) very satisfied" (Keith, 1985). Higher scores on both questions represented more positive assessments. *Perceived economic well-being since divorce* was measured by the question: "Since my divorce, I believe I am: (1) more economically well-off; (2) just as economically well-off; (3) not quite as economically well-off; and (4) much worse-off economically." The responses to the question on perceived economic well-being since divorce were listed in reverse order to avoid a set pattern of responses. The order was again reversed when the data were coded so all measures would reflect higher scores for positive assessments.

Administration of the Instrument

Because our target population is difficult to identify in the general population, a non-probability sample was drawn. Potential organizations with the largest memberships, i.e., more than 20, listed in the *Directory of Singles Organizations of the Greater Baton Rouge Area* were chosen for participation in the study. Leaders of the largest groups were telephoned to get permission to distribute and collect questionnaires at a regularly scheduled meeting of the group. A total of 186 completed questionnaires were collected from four religious and five secular single's organizations. Fifty individuals were eliminated from these analyses because they were either separated, widowed, or did not indicate their marital status. Of the resulting 136 divorced individuals, 49 were males, 80 females. Seven did not indicate their gender.

Sample Characteristics

Respondent's mean age was 43.85 years; mean educational level was 14.8 years for males and 14.1 for females; mean years divorced were 5.47; and mean income was in the $20,000 to $24,999 range. Fifty-seven (73.1%) of the females and 44 (95.7%) of the males were employed prior to divorce. Ninety-five (89.6%) of the respondents neither paid nor received child support. Only 51 (37.5%) of the respondents reported having physical custody of children.

Data Analyses

Spearman's rho was used to determine the correlations among perceived financial adequacy, satisfaction with level of living, and perceived economic well-being since divorce. Chi-square analyses were used to determine whether receipt of assistance was related to perceived financial adequacy, satisfaction with level of living, and perceived economic well-being since divorce. Due to the ordered, categorical nature of the dependent variables, logistic regression was used to determine the relationship between each of the dependent variables and the independent variables. Logistic regression was also used to determine the relationship between receipt of assistance and the selected independent variables. Thus, responses to receipt of assistance were collapsed into two categories: received assistance and had not received assistance. All analyses were performed using SAS® system. All hypotheses were tested at $\alpha = .05$.

RESULTS

Although the majority of the sample reported positive responses on financial adequacy (87.5%), most were dissatisfied with perceived level of living (63.9%) and were economically worse-off perceptually (56.2%) since their divorce. Logistic regression was used to determine which independent variables were related to each of the dependent variables. Income and having physical custody of children were significantly related to perceptions of financial adequacy. Only income was also significantly related to satisfaction with level of living. Both findings are consistent with the findings of others. Perceived economic well-being was significantly related only to the number of years divorced.

Spearman rank correlation was used to determine the relationships among perceived financial adequacy, satisfaction with level of living, and perceived economic well-being since divorce. Significant correlations were found among all three components of overall economic well-being.

Assistance

Most of the respondents (63.2%, n = 86) reported receiving no assistance from family and friends. Only 50 (36.8%) respondents reported receiving assistance of some kind.

Logistic regression was used to determine whether selected independent variables were useful in explaining receipt of assistance. Age was the only significant variable in this model $\chi^2(1, N = 81) = 5.90, p < .01$. Younger divorcees were more likely to receive assistance.

Type of Assistance

Forty (29.4%) of the respondents received services, with babysitting the most frequently reported service ($n = 22$, 16.2%) (see Table 1). The number of respondents receiving the other services were, in order: chauffeuring of child (n = 16, 11.8%), help with household chores (n = 13, 9.6%), laundry services (n = 12, 8.8%), and transportation assistance (n = 10, 7.4%). The number of respondents who reported receiving goods was 33 (24.3%). The most frequently received good was clothing (n = 22, 22.7%). Food was received by 21 (15.4%) of the respondents, and household necessities were received by 12 (8.8%) of the respondents. Only 16.2% (n = 22) of the sample reported receiving money.

Chi-square analyses were used to determine whether males and

TABLE 1. Number and Percentage of Types of Assistance Received by Respondents

Type of assistance	n[a]		%	
Services	40[b]		29.4	
Babysitting		22		16.2
Chauffeuring of child		16		11.8
Household chores		13		9.6
Laundry		12		8.8
Transportation		10		7.4
Goods	33[b]		24.3	
Clothes		22		16.2
Food		21		15.4
Household necessities		12		8.8
Money	22[b]		16.2	

Note. N = 136.
[a]Respondents could check more than one item in any category, therefore n varies for specific types of goods and services.
[b]Total number reporting receipt of all types of services, goods, or money.

females differed in the types of assistance they received. Results showed that females received significantly more goods χ^2 (1, N = 129) = 6.73, $p < .01$, and money, χ^2 (1, N = 129) = 6.68, $p < .01$, than males received. There was no difference in the receipt of services by sex.

Frequency of Assistance

Although very few respondents received assistance often (i.e., daily), services were received more frequently by both sexes than either goods or money. Females received child-related services more frequently than males.

Goods. Clothes (n = 22) were more frequently received than any other type of goods. Most received clothes less than monthly, but one reported receiving clothes daily. Next, respondents received food (n = 18) most often monthly, but one received food daily. Household necessities were received by a few (n = 10), less than monthly.

Money. Money was received by 15.4% (n = 21) of the respondents, most often on a less than monthly basis, but one received money daily.

Service. Babysitting (n = 20) was the service most frequently received and most often, monthly. The second most frequently received service was chauffeuring (n = 15) of a child, equally often for daily or less than monthly basis. Laundry service (n = 11) and help with household chores (n = 10) were received weekly. Transportation was received daily by only one respondent with a few (n = 6) reporting infrequent transportation service.

Receipt of Assistance to Dependent Variables

Using the Chi-square statistic the receipt of assistance was found to be significantly related to satisfaction with level of living, χ^2 (1, N = 87) = 6.906, $p < .01$, but not to perceived financial adequacy or economic well-being. Individuals who scored higher on satisfaction with level of living received less assistance than those who scored lower on satisfaction with level of living.

DISCUSSION

Most of the respondents reported positive answers for perceived financial adequacy; that is, they were able to get along reasonably well on the income available. Considering that most of our sample, both males and females, were employed (73% of females and 96% of males) prior to divorce, that the average educational level was more than two years of college for both genders, and the mean income was above $20,000, this sample was unlike that expected randomly. Two other unique aspects of the sample, which may help to explain financial adequacy responses, are that only 10% either paid or received support and 62.57% did not have physical custody of the children. Indeed, as might be expected, divorcees who perceived their finances as inadequate were more likely to have physical custody of children and/or to have lower incomes. Divorcees with children at home had larger households, thus greater financial needs and wants, than divorcees without dependents. When economic and demographic variables were taken into account, there were no differences found between men and women in their perceptions of financial adequacy, yet more women reported negative changes in income following divorce than did men.

Ability to manage on the income available was not synonymous with satisfaction with standard of living. Divorcees seemed aware of and sensitive to the drop in financial resources resulting in a lower level of living.

The only significant predictor for economic well-being since divorce was years divorced. This may be due to improvement in the divorcee's economic situation, learning management skills, or cognitive dissonance.

Although the effects of lowered income seem detrimental to the divorced individual's ability to survive financially and to the divorced individual's financial satisfaction, the effects appear to diminish over time. Perhaps economic well-being also can be predicted by subjective, complex items, such as management skills, attitudes, or self-esteem.

The majority of divorcees in this sample did not receive practical assistance from family or friends. However, younger respondents were much more likely to receive assistance than older respondents.

Assistance was more likely to be in the form of service, since younger people are more likely to have dependent children and, therefore, a greater need for assistance. Many of the respondents, both male and female, received infrequent assistance with child-related services, such as babysitting and chauffeuring of child. The fact that females received goods and money more often than the male respondents, may be related to families' responses to females' lower incomes, having children at home, and socialization of the sexes toward acceptance of help.

As adults, we are usually socialized to become independent. Therefore, when we must receive assistance to maintain a certain level of living, we may react with negative attitudes.

The implications of these findings for professionals who may have an impact on divorcees, such as family counselors and policy makers, are that divorcees, as well as other single parents, could benefit from aid aimed at helping them manage financially with being a single parent. Although not addressed in this study, it is well known that custodial parents often do not receive very much financial assistance from the noncustodial parent. Even if he/she is supposed to receive child support, he/she often does not receive the full amount of the support (Bureau of the Census, 1989; Halem, 1982). Enforcing child support payments and impressing on the paying parents how necessary the payments are would benefit custodial parents, not to mention the children involved. The divorcee with children may also be in need of affordable daycare to feel that he/she can manage on income available.

Those divorcees with low incomes may need help in discovering financial alternatives, such as going back to school with public aid, acquiring a roommate if housing costs are high, or developing interview skills to get a better paying job. Since recent divorcees felt their economic well-being to be lower, counselors can point out to them that as single persons they have more control over their finances, and that with good management skills their situations can improve with time. Good management skills also may improve the divorcee's ability to get along on income available and increase financial satisfaction.

The findings of this study may indicate that families are less likely to offer assistance to adult children who are divorced than to adult children marrying for the first time. Although divorce is more common and more accepted today, attitudes of families may be different about providing assistance to the first time married child than to the divorced child. Replication of this study with different socioeconomic levels and races with a larger, random sample could add to the information on interfamily grants for other demographic groups.

REFERENCES

Ackerman, N., & Paolucci, B. (1983). Objective and subjective income adequacy: Their relationship to perceived life quality measures. *Social Indicators Research, 12*(1), 25-48.

Adams, J. J., & Adams, N. W. (1979). *Divorce: How and when to let go*. Englewood Cliffs, New Jersey: Prentice-Hall.

Albrecht, S. L. (1980). Reactions and adjustments to divorce: Differences in the experiences of males and females. *Family Relations, 29*, 59-68.

Albrecht, S. L., Bahr, H. M., & Goodman, K. L. (1983). *Divorce and remarriage: Problems, adaptations and adjustments*. Westport, Connecticut: Greenwood Press.

Amato, P. R., & Partridge, S. (1987). Widows and divorcees with dependent children: Material, personal, family, and social well-being. *Family Relations, 36*, 316-320.

Bahr, S. J. (1983). Marital dissolution laws: Impact of recent changes for women. *Journal of Family Issues, 4*(3), 455-466.

Bauer, J. W., & Hogan, M. J. (1987). Family financial management: Theory and research findings. *Proceedings of the 1987 Family Economics-Home Management Preconference Workshop.*

Berardo, D. H. (1982). Divorce and remarriage at middle age and beyond. *Annals of the American Academy of Political and Social Sciences, 464*, 132-139.

Bohannon, P. (1970). The six stations of divorce. In P. Bohanon (Ed.), *Divorce and After* (pp. 25-55). Garden City, New York: Doubleday.

Bureau of the Census. (1989). *Child support and alimony: 1985* (Supplemental Report, Current Population Reports, Series P-23, No. 154). Washington, D.C.: U.S. Government Printing Office.

Clark, A. B., & Warren, J. (1963). Economic contributions made to newly married couples by their parents. Cornell University, Agricultural Experiment Station, Ithaca, New York.

Corcoran, M. (1979). The economic consequences of marital dissolution for women in the middle years. *Sex Roles, 5*(3), 343-353.

Day, R. D., & Bahr, S. J. (1986). Income changes following divorce and remarriage. *Journal of Divorce, 9*(3), 75-88.

Duncan, G. J., & Hoffman, S. D. (1985). A reconsideration of the economic consequences of marital dissolution. *Demography, 22*(4), 485-497.

Espenshade, T. J. (1979). The economic consequences of divorce. *Journal of Marriage and the Family, 41*(3), 615-625.

Gander, A., & Jorgensen, L. (1990). Post divorce adjustment: Social supports among older divorced persons. *Journal of Divorce, 13*(4), 37-52.

Gerstel, N. (1988). Divorce and kin ties: The impact of gender. *Journal of Marriage and the Family, 50*(1), 209-219.

Goode, W. J. (1956). *Women in divorce*. Westport, Connecticut: Greenwood Press.

Hagestad, G. O., & Smyer, M. A. (1982). Dissolving long-term relationships: Patterns of divorcing in middle age. In S. Duck (Ed.), *Personal relationships. 4: Dissolving personal relationships* (pp. 155-188). New York: Academic Press.

Halem, L. C. (1982). *Separated and divorced women*. Westport, Connecticut: Greenwood Press.

Hampton, R. (1975). Marital disruption: Some social and economic consequences. In G. J. Duncan and J. N. Morgan (Eds.), *Five thousand American families–patterns of economic progress* (Vol. 3, pp. 163-186). Ann Arbor, Michigan: University of Michigan, Institute for Social Research.

Hennon, C. B. (1983). Divorce and the elderly: A neglected area of research. In T. H. Brubaker (Ed.), *Family relationships in later life* (pp. 149-172). Beverly Hills: Sage.

Hoffman, S. (1977). Marital instability and the economic status of women. *Demography, 14*(1), 67-76.

Hoffman, S., & Holmes, J. (1976). Husbands, wives, and divorce. In G. J. Duncan & J. N. Morgan (Eds.), *Five thousand American families–patterns of economic progress* (Vol. 4, pp. 23-76). Ann Arbor, Michigan: University of Michigan, Institute for Social Research.

Johnson, C. L. (1988). Postdivorce reorganization of relationships between divorcing children and their parents. *Journal of Marriage and the Family, 50*(1), 221-231.

Keith, P. M. (1985). Financial well-being of older divorced/separated men and women: Findings from a panel study. *Journal of Divorce, 9*(1), 61-72.

Mauldin, T. (1991). Economic consequences of divorce or separation among women in poverty. *Journal of Divorce & Remarriage, 14*, 162-177.

McCullagh, P. (1980). Regression models for ordinal data. *Journal of the Royal Statistical Society, 42*(2), 109-142.

National Center for Health Statistics. (1988). *Vital Statistics of the United States, 1984, Vol. III, Marriage and Divorce* (DHHS Publication No. PHS 88-1103). Washington, D.C.: U.S. Government Printing Office.

Rowe, B. R. (1989). The economics of divorce. *Proceedings of the 1989 Family Economics-Home Management Preconference Workshop*, 89-99.

Strong, B., DeVault, C., Suid, M., & Reynolds, R. (1983). *The Marriage and Family Experience* (2nd Ed.) St. Paul, Minnesota: West Publishing.

U. S. Department of Commerce. (1990). *Statistical Abstract of the United States* (110th ed.). Current Population Reports. Washington, D.C.: Bureau of the Census.

Weiss, R. S. (1984). The impact of marital dissolution on income and consumption in single-parent households. *Journal of Marriage and the Family, 46*(1), 115-127.

Weitzman, L. (1985). *The divorce revolution: The unexpected social and economic consequences for women and children in America.* New York: Free Press.

Economic Consequences of Marital Dissolution

Atlee L. Stroup
Gene E. Pollock

SUMMARY. This study analyzes Weitzman's suggestion that men average a 42 percent gain and women a 73 percent decline in standard of living in the first year after divorce. A cross-sectional GSS data set of white respondents for 1983-87 is used. Family incomes of divorced women and men are compared with their married counterparts for five SES categories. For both genders, incomes of divorced persons are lower than incomes of married persons. Family incomes are regressed against a set of control variables and a marital status variable. The marital status variable was statistically significant in determining family incomes for both genders.

Divorce demands social, psychological, economic and other adjustments. Common sense, clinical references, and conclusions from a variety of studies lead one to the conclusion that the economic arena of post-divorce adjustment is an important one, and that women are more vulnerable than men. For many observers, divorce is related causally to the increase in single parent homes

---

Atlee L. Stroup, PhD, is Professor Emeritus of Sociology, and Gene E. Pollock, PhD, is Professor of Economics, both at The College of Wooster, Wooster, OH.

This paper represents a revised version of one presented at the annual meeting of the National Council on Family Relations, Orlando, FL, November, 1992.

[Haworth co-indexing entry note]: "Economic Consequences of Marital Dissolution." Stroup, Atlee L., and Gene E. Pollock. Co-published simultaneously in *Journal of Divorce & Remarriage* (The Haworth Press, Inc.) Vol. 22, No. 1/2, 1994, pp. 37-54; and: *The Economics of Divorce: The Effects on Parents and Children* (ed: Craig A. Everett) The Haworth Press, Inc., 1994, pp. 37-54. Multiple copies of this article/chapter may be purchased from The Haworth Document Delivery Center [1-800-3-HAWORTH; 9:00 a.m. - 5:00 p.m. (EST)].

and "the feminization of poverty" (Ehrenreich and Piven, 1984). One author, Lenore Weitzman, in an important work, *The Divorce Revolution*, holds that the aftermath of divorce for women has been more harmful in the last two decades than was true in previous years. In this work the author suggests that the economic well-being of divorced women (and their children) suffered typically a sharp decline after the enactment of "no-fault" divorce laws in the various states. Traditionally, being allowed to argue from an "innocent" position, the wife could bargain for economic advantage and often obtain alimony. While theoretically the no-fault concept was to proceed from a working assumption of equity, in practice women lost their bargaining power in the new system and were left comparatively vulnerable. Weitzman (1985: 323) suggests, " . . . that when income is compared to needs, divorced men experience an average 42 percent rise in their standard of living in the first year after the divorce, while divorced women (and their children) experience a 73 percent decline."

Weitzman's work has been criticized for its geographic, social class and other limitations (Okin, 1991; Hoffman and Duncan, 1988). The sample was limited to a particular geographic area of California, a state somewhat unique culturally, and a community property state. It is clear that a number of variables, not just development and implementation of the no-fault concept, are involved in changes in divorce procedures and in the status of females in society. While the consequences of no-fault divorce are no doubt substantial, this paper will not attempt to determine these consequences. The suggestion in the literature that divorced women are presently much more vulnerable economically than divorced men has important implications for divorced women and women approaching divorce. Furthermore, since a majority of children of divorce are under custody of the mother, the implications of the above are important for the welfare of the children also.

It is our intention in this paper to assess the economic situation of divorced women and divorced men in a sizeable sample based on a cross-sectional population drawn from a major survey. If major economic disparities are systematically occurring between divorced women and divorced men in their economic situations over the nation, they should evidence themselves in national survey reports.

Before turning to this particular study's approach, attention to some background literature is in order.

BACKGROUND

Measurement of Economic Impact of Divorce

The researcher who attempts to assess the literature on the economic impact of divorce and who attempts to make comparisons between studies encounters basic theoretical and practical problems. First, some reports are based on longitudinal studies and some on cross-sectional ones. Second, definitions of the criterion variable vary considerably. Current income level, drop in income, drop in "expected income," and negative income events are often used. A number of researchers now use a concept of "need" in reference to standard of living (Weitzman, 1985); (Hoffman and Duncan, 1988). As Okin (1991) points out, these two often quoted studies do not adjust income for need in the same fashion. These two studies, along with many others, are not strictly comparable. At present a standard "adjusted need" measure does not exist. The measure used in this study is family income coded into categories.

Socioeconomic Status

Another major issue, from the social-scientific point of view, is social status or social class. In many studies the socioeconomic status of the subjects is not clearly indicated. The stratification literature suggests that family life varies considerably by SES level. If this is basic, it surely applies in divorce adjustment. Commenting on this sharply is Ambert (1989). Noting that over the years many studies have indicated the importance of SES in social situations, she finds that few studies on divorce outcome control for this variable. The author states that " . . . it is entirely possible that some of the results of studies on divorce are misleading and generalizations inappropriate because of this lack of control for SES" (1989:12).

Determinants of Divorce

We assume that with the end of marriage in sight, negotiations of some type begin between the respective spouses. For the childless couple, issues of property settlement and possible spousal support are central. When children are involved, questions of child support, custody, and visitation rights are added. Educational level should theoretically affect the ability of each individual to assess the legal aspects of the divorce system and long-term implications of economic agreements, joint custody, support arrangements, legal sanctions, and other issues. Further, educational level is associated with ability to compete in the labor market. Education and the ability to compete in the labor market are associated with higher levels of adjustment (Spanier and Thompson, 1984; Steil and Weltman, 1991).

For both men and women, number of dependent children is important. As Teachman and Polonko (1990) point out, the popular conceptual model of divorce negotiation outcome is that of mother receiving child custody, father receiving visitation rights and child support obligations, and marital property being divided. They suggest that in actual practice, the model is somewhat modified and divorce law and court practice cannot be overlooked. The literature clearly suggests the child support payments by males are inadequate, inconsistent, and in a proportion of cases, non-existent. Teachman (1990), Weitzman (1985) and Arendell (1986) and many others refer to difficulties encountered by divorced mothers in their attempts to balance employment, supervision, and general undergirding and care of minor children.

Another variable to be considered is that of hours worked outside the home in the labor force. The divorced person, especially in the poorer classes and with responsibility for child care, must either receive considerable financial support from the ex-spouse, other family members, governmental transfer payments, or a combination of these. Usually such support is inadequate for the individual's standard of living and the divorcee attempts to work full time in the marketplace. Many such parents, and especially females, express feelings of isolation and the sense of "overwhelming responsibilities" when reflecting on this situation (Wattenberg and Reinhardt, 1979:464). Working extra hours or at two jobs is not uncommon (Arendell, 1986:60).

Age is a variable to be considered here. With divorce becoming more common in the last two decades, more middle-aged and older persons are involved in divorce than would have been predicted in former periods. This has been especially difficult for traditional females who, with no-fault divorce, are forced to enter or re-enter the work force (Okin, 1991). Both Corcoran (1979) and Morgan (1991), focusing on mid-life women, found significant decline in economic circumstance for divorced women in their sample who had not remarried, as a whole. Most studies of divorcees find women in more precarious situations than men, but not all do. Keith (1985) finds older divorced men to be objectively in better economic circumstances than divorced females, but subjectively, the men were more negative than the women with regard to perceived economic status.

From another point of view, both Duncan and Morgan (1976) and Day and Bahr (1986) suggest that older persons will have a competitive advantage due to education, training and work history. Morgan (1991:24) argues that surveys tend to find younger divorcees to be more disadvantaged than their older divorced sisters, when compared to married women.

Gender Differences

The literature in the economic aspects of post-divorce is reasonably consistent. There is general agreement that divorced women have increased financial stress after divorce, with a sharp decline in income: Hoffman (1977); Albrecht (1980); Braver et al., (1989); Kitson and Morgan (1990). Most of the above report a female income decline of about 30% with divorce, a sharp drop, but one out of line with Weitzman's reported 73%. A number of studies make references to recent changes in divorce procedure, including reductions in alimony or spousal support.

The literature discussing the impact of divorce on men is less consistent than for women. Hoffman (1977) found that for the 1968-74 period, "real" income for divorced women decreased by 29.3% while that for divorced men decreased 19.2%. Adjusting for family "needs," divorced women had a 6.7% reduction while divorced men achieved a 16.5% increase.

Duncan and Hoffman (1985), using a five-year period to focus on family income, found that for divorced/separated women, the ratio of family income during the fifth year of divorce to the last year of marriage was 1.01 whereas for men it was 1.14.

In the Day and Bahr (1986) survey, male divorcees suffered an initial drop in per capita family income; they then recovered and by five years post-divorce had outpaced divorced women "substantially." Their results indicate that when number of children are controlled, median per capita family income for divorced females is about 64% of that of married females, whereas for divorced males, it is 96% of that of married males.

METHODS

Sample

Data used in this study are drawn from the General Social Surveys done by the Chicago-based National Public Opinion Research Center's General Social Surveys. While local populations of divorced or separated persons can and should be researched, they often reflect particular cultural characteristics and they typically involve a small base N. The NORC attempts to obtain each year a stratified, national probability sample which is representative of major segments of the society of the United States.

Sampling design and procedure can be found in the appendix of any NORC codebook (Davis and Smith, 1989). On a yearly basis, a sample of roughly 1500 English speaking adults, eighteen and over, are drawn and subjected to an extensive interview procedure by a trained staff of interviewers. While the interviewer schedules change somewhat from year to year, a core set of basic items and questions carry over from year to year. This results in a cumulative record which can be tapped, thus allowing both longitudinal comparison and the development of large data bases for use in analysis. For this study the years 1983 through 1987 were combined, allowing us to compare the economic well-being of a sizeable sub-sample of separated or divorced persons with that of their married cohorts.

Specific Design

This study is based then on a cross-sectional approach. A number of the divorce impact studies have used a longitudinal design. These are important and should be continued, but it should be recognized that they often have important problems. These include panel loss, reinterview bias, and the difficulty of determining period and cohort effects (Menard, 1991). Seldom do longitudinal studies reflect the major geographic and socioeconomic strata of the total society as does the GSS data base.

In terms of design, we will move through a series of steps to illustrate the relationship between marital status (married and divorced and/or separated) and family income. (Hereafter divorced and/or separated will be referred to as divorced.) Along with these two main variables, attention will be focused on a series of independent variables to be used as controls. These are educational level (EDUC), age (AGE), hours worked in the labor force (HOURS), size of household (HOMPOP) and socioeconomic level (OCC). In the first stage of analysis, mean differences in family income for the divorced-separated vs. married (hereafter labeled Marital) will be delineated and analyzed by a t-test procedure to determine if the two groups have significant differences in family income. This will be done for the total sample and for each of five SES (OCC) categories. In the second stage of analysis, a two-step regression approach will be used. In the first step, the main control variables of educational level, hours worked, household size, and age will be entered as a block, as predictors and determinants of the dependent variable family income. In the second step, the dummy variable, marital status, will be added to the equation. Focus here will first be on the total sample, by sex. In this paper only white respondents will be used. Then separate runs will be made and results presented for each of the five SES categories.

Results

At the top in Table 1 is the comparison of the divorced females with married females on mean income, with ratio and t-test results given. As can be seen, divorced women in the sample have significantly lower mean family incomes than the married women. The ratio of divorced to married is .78, indicating a "loss" of 22%. This is not as low as the roughly 30% gap of the major studies. The gap between the two mean income levels is far different from what would be projected from the Weitzman 73% drop generalization. Note, then, the breakdown by five SES categories. The mean levels

TABLE 1. Comparison of Mean Income, for White Females, by Marital Status and SES, 1983-'87 GSS Data.

SES Category	Marital Status	Mean Income[a]	N[b]	Ratio[c]	t-Value	Significance[d]
Total-All	Divorced	8.36	533			
SES	Married	10.73	1847	.78	–16.84	.000
1. Professional, Technical	Divorced	10.17	78			
	Married	11.51	315	.88	–5.40	.000
2. Executive, Admin, Sales	Divorced	8.93	250			
	Married	11.12	871	.80	–12.00	.000
3. Crafts	Divorced	8.93	14			
	Married	10.47	59	.85	–1.89	.079
4. Operatives	Divorced	7.44	54			
	Married	9.72	134	.77	–5.53	.000
5. Unskilled Labor	Divorced	7.08	114			
	Married	10.12	317	.70	–9.18	.000

a. Income is family income coded into categories: 1 = under $1,000; 2 = 1,000 to 2,999; 3 = 3,000 to 3,999; 4 = 4,000 to 4,999; 5 = 5,000 to 5,999; 6 = 6,000 to 6,999; 7 = 7,000 to 7,999; 8 = 8,000 to 9,999; 9 = 9,000 to 14,999; 10 = 15,000 to 19,999; 11 = 20,000 to 24,999; 12 = 25,000 and over.

b. A pair wise approach (cases with complete data for the relationship) was used for all four tables.

c. Ratio of divorced mean income to married mean income.

d. Separate variance estimate, 2-tail probability level of significance.

for the divorced are consistently lower than for the married, and significant at all levels but number three. (The latter level has a small N which probably explains the lack of significance.) As Morgan (1990:95) stresses, the "characteristics" of the women substantially influence the economic consequences of marriage ending. She states that "those with the highest incomes . . . still maintained higher economic well-being and lower rates of poverty than women who had ended their marriages in very marginal or poverty level circumstances." Note the top two classes of divorced have means of 10.17 and 8.93 compared to the 7.44 and 7.08 of the two lower SES levels, a sharp comparative difference.

Table 2 contains a similar breakdown for men. Keeping in mind the suggestion of Weitzman and others of economic gain by males with divorce, the results are sharply contrary to expectations. First, for the total male sample, we note a divorced mean income of 9.72 and a married one of 10.83 with a ratio of the former to the latter of .90. While this "loss" or gap is only 10% compared to the female 22% of Table 1, it is sharply different from Weitzman's suggestion of a "gain" of 42%. As we scan the results for the various SES categories, we note that the differences between the divorced and married men are significant in all five cases. On a comparative basis, the upper two categories of divorced men clearly are superior in average income to the lower two categories, although the gap between the two is not as pronounced as it is for females.

To establish the determinants of income, multiple regression was used. Four variables were used as controls–education level, hours worked outside the home, age, and number of persons in the household. The last variable which is of most importance for this study is a marital variable (divorced vs. married) which is a dummy variable assigned the value of 1 for divorced and 0 for married. In Tables 3 and 4 results are presented for females and males, in order. A two-step approach was used, with the four major control variables entered as a block in step 1 against income as the dependent variable. In step 2, the dummy variable marital (divorced vs. married) was added. Focusing on the female total sample in Table 3 (top) one notes that, by Beta weight, t-value and significance level, the education and household size variables stand out in their weights and/or contribution to the equation, although hours worked and age are

TABLE 2. Comparison of Mean Income, for White Males, by Marital Status and SES, 1983-'87 GSS Data.

SES Category	Marital Status	Mean Income[a]	N[b]	Ratio[c]	t-Value	Significance[d]
Total-All	Divorced	9.72	279			
SES	Married	10.83	1718	.90	–6.07	.000
1. Professional, Technical	Divorced	10.64	47			
	Married	11.57	308	.92	–2.35	.023
2. Executive, Admin, Sales	Divorced	10.33	88			
	Married	11.23	529	.92	–2.95	.004
3. Crafts	Divorced	9.60	65			
	Married	10.65	389	.90	–3.14	.002
4. Operatives	Divorced	8.25	28			
	Married	10.19	151	.81	–2.76	.010
5. Unskilled Labor	Divorced	8.78	51			
	Married	10.09	335	.87	–3.03	.004

a. Income is family income coded into categories: 1 = under $1,000; 2 = 1,000 to 2,999; 3 = 3,000 to 3,999; 4 = 4,000 to 4,999; 5 = 5,000 to 5,999; 6 = 6,000 to 6,999; 7 = 7,000 to 7,999; 8 = 8,000 to 9,999; 9 = 9,000 to 14,999; 10 = 15,000 to 19,999; 11 = 20,000 to 24,999; 12 = 25,000 and over.
b. A pair wise approach (cases with complete data for the relationship) was used for all four tables.
c. Ratio of divorced mean income to married mean income.
d. Separate variance estimate, 2-tail probability level of significance.

significant. The R^2 is a modest .127. When the marital status variable is added, the household size contribution is reduced and age fades to insignificance. Marital status and education make the greatest contributions. The R^2 level reaches .26, sharply higher than the (.127) level of step 1. All signs are in the expected direction except in the case of household size, and household size is only significant for the total sample size and two out of five of the SES categories. Proceeding from SES 1 to 5, the results are reasonably consistent. Education and household size tend to stand out compared to hours worked and age in step 1, but in SES level 3 no variable is significant. This probably reflects small sample size.

In Table 4, for males the total sample, education, hours worked and household size all stand out as making a significant contribution in step 1, with age being insignificant. The R^2 is close to that for females, .139. When the marital status variable is added in step 2, education and hours worked remain significant, with household size no longer being significant. Notice that, with the controls, marital status still makes a significant and important contribution to the equation. The R^2 change from .139 in step 1 to .161 in step 2 is a modest one compared to the change for women.

In the subcategories of SES, it is clear that education and hours worked are generally significant, whereas the contribution of household size is less consistent. Regarding this variable, it is in step 1 significant in four of five levels, but significant at only the highest SES level in step 2 when marital is included. Household size tends to be important at the upper level of social class 1 and 2 for females, and 1 for males, but not at lower levels. In the higher SES levels financial support for both divorced women and divorced men may be more likely to be available. The availability of this support may account for the positive signs and significance of the household size variable in the regression runs for higher SES levels. The data set did not contain a control variable for this financial support. Therefore, this explanation could not be tested empirically.

CONCLUSION

1. Weitzman's reference to a 73% loss of income for divorced females appears to be high. The figure of 30% would seem to be

TABLE 3. Regression of Income on Control Variables (Step 1) Plus Marital Status (Step 2), by Total Sample and SES Category, 1983-'87 GSS Data, White Female Respondents.

		STEP 1			STEP 2		
SES Category	Variable	Beta	t-Value	Sig.	Beta	t-Value	Sig.
Total	Educ	.300	11.29	.000	.281	11.49	.000
	Hours	.067	2.51	.012	.116	4.69	.000
	Age	.069	2.45	.015	.013	.50	.616
	Hh	.214	7.60	.000	.102	3.78	.002
	Marital				–.387	–15.42	.000
	R^2	.127			.262		
1.	Educ	.278	4.69	.000	.244	4.30	.000
	Hours	–.001	–.02	.986	.026	.45	.650
	Age	–.053	–.88	.380	–.097	–1.68	.094
	Hh	.219	3.62	.000	.138	2.31	.021
	Marital				–.298	–5.13	.000
	R^2	.142			.221		
2.	Educ	.140	3.78	.000	.139	4.15	.000
	Hours	.097	2.60	.009	.175	5.12	.000
	Age	.084	2.16	.031	.023	.66	.512
	Hh	.291	7.45	.000	.170	4.66	.000
	Marital				–.439	–12.59	.000
	R^2	.089			.258		

3.	Educ	.256	1.51	.141	.241	1.43	.164
	Hours	.226	1.47	.152	.183	1.16	.254
	Age	–.180	–.98	.337	–.249	–1.29	.208
	Hh	.252	1.48	.149	.120	.58	.564
	Marital				–.207	–1.14	.262
	R^2	.336			.364		
4.	Educ	.176	1.55	.125	.179	1.69	.094
	Hours	.266	2.59	.011	.312	3.25	.002
	Age	.128	.99	.321	.052	.43	.668
	Hh	.229	2.02	.047	.055	.48	.630
	Marital				–.390	–3.84	.000
	R^2	.146			.273		
5.	Educ	.196	2.87	.005	.189	3.07	.002
	Hours	–.012	–.18	.856	.034	.57	.572
	Age	.008	.10	.919	–.012	–.18	.855
	Hh	.214	2.93	.004	.100	1.48	.142
	Marital				–.431	–7.12	.000
	R^2	.093			.263		

TABLE 4. Regression of Income on Control Variables (Step 1) Plus Marital Status (Step 2) by Total Sample and SES Categories, 1983-'87 GSS Data, White Male Respondents.

		STEP 1			STEP 2		
SES Category	Variable	Beta	t-Value	Sig.	Beta	t-Value	Sig.
Total	Educ	.296	12.13	.000	.294	12.20	.000
	Hours	.140	5.82	.000	.145	6.06	.000
	Age	.011	.44	.658	−.017	−.68	.495
	Hh	.112	4.50	.000	.045	1.69	.092
	Marital				−.161	−6.27	.000
	R^2	.139			.161		
1.	Educ	.226	4.08	.000	.217	3.91	.000
	Hours	.109	1.96	.051	.106	1.91	.057
	Age	.012	.21	.838	−.012	−.22	.830
	Hh	.184	3.22	.001	.131	2.09	.037
	Marital				−.123	−2.02	.045
	R^2	.110			.122		
2.	Educ	.196	4.46	.000	.207	4.76	.000
	Hours	.154	3.48	.001	.156	3.59	.000
	Age	.028	.61	.544	−.005	−.11	.910
	Hh	.080	1.78	.076	−.006	−.13	.897
	Marital				−.185	−3.90	.000
	R^2	.081			.108		

3.	Educ	.180	3.15	.002	.176	3.13	.002
	Hours	.128	2.32	.021	.146	2.68	.008
	Age	.000	.00	.998	–.033	–.54	.587
	Hh	.113	1.95	.052	.043	.70	.486
	Marital				–.183	–3.13	.002
	R^2	.068			.096		
4.	Educ	.238	2.78	.006	.251	2.99	.003
	Hours	.287	3.43	.001	.279	3.41	.001
	Age	–.041	–.45	.656	–.047	–.53	.595
	Hh	.178	2.01	.047	.085	.91	.367
	Marital				–.232	–2.62	.010
	R^2	.204			.249		
5.	Educ	.262	4.31	.000	.257	4.28	.000
	Hours	.120	2.08	.038	.124	2.18	.030
	Age	–.007	–.11	.912	–.045	–.71	.481
	Hh	.118	1.99	.047	.054	.87	.386
	Marital				–.172	–2.85	.005
	R^2	.113			.138		

more reasonable based on a number of studies in this field using different methodologies. The gap between our divorced women's income and married women's income would be slightly smaller than this figure, but the gap is there. It is important to focus on SES as well, rather than grouping all women together into one category. Using a comparative approach, one can say, with Morgan (1991:96) that "to a large extent economic consequences following the departure from marriage depend on characteristics and decisions that shaped the woman's life long before the marriage ended." Those that start low remain low, and the reverse.

2. The sharp generalization of a 42 percent rise in living standards for males certainly does not hold for our sample. Instead, the men experience about a 10% drop in average income. This represents probably the most important outcome of this research. Divorced women are more vulnerable than divorced men economically, but for this sample divorced men's economic circumstances are slightly below their peers who are married. This holds for each level of SES.

3. It is clear that Weitzman's generalizations do not hold for this population studied. They remain widely cited in textbooks and the media (Cox, 1987:511; Skolnick, 1987:281). The modern media approach of generalizations without detailed breakdown may be socializing a consumer public to this mode of discourse. If so, it is imperative that results be based on clear-cut definitions of variables, proper samples, and methods of analysis which delineate as carefully as possible the determinants and the consequences. This study used a national probability sample and attempted to measure the significance of marital status on incomes of married and divorced persons while controlling for other variables which are also determinants of income. Marital status was shown to be an important determinant of income.

4. Moving further at the policy level, financial undergirding of children is very much at issue here. Since the mid-seventies the various states have adopted their own versions of the Uniform Reciprocal Enforcement of Support Act, and have set up their own systems to require those divorced parents (primarily fathers) to follow local court orders of child support for which they are responsible. These efforts are only partially successful, as is generally

understood. Presently in a number of states, including Ohio, efforts are being made to (1) establish paternity and implied economic responsibility outside of marriage, and (2) enforce child support more strictly. This movement is backed by an uneasy alliance between some liberals and conservatives. There is a general assumption that most absent fathers "could contribute significant amounts of child support" (Goldberg, 1992). The data in this study would suggest that such an assumption may be an over-simplification if divorced men are not as able to pay as Weitzman's study would indicate.

REFERENCES

Albrecht, S. (1980). Reactions and adjustments to divorce: Differences in the experiences of males and females. *Family Relations*, 29, 59-68.

Ambert, A. (1989). A study of relationships. Connecticut: Jai Press, Inc.

Arendell, Terry. (1986). Mothers and divorce. Berkeley, CA: University of California Press.

Braver, S.L. et al. (1989). Economic hardship and psychological distress in custodial mothers. *Journal of Divorce*, 6, 19-33.

Corcoran, M.E. (1979). The economic consequences of marital dissolution for women in the middle years. *Sex Roles*, 5, 343-353.

Cox, F. (1987). Human intimacy: Marriage, the family, and its meaning. St. Paul, MN: West.

Davis, J. & Smith, T. (1989). General social surveys, 1972-1989: Cumulative codebook. Chicago, National Opinion Research Center, University of Chicago.

Day, R. & Bahr, S.J. (1986). Income changes following divorce and remarriage. *Journal of Divorce*, 3, 75-88.

Duncan, G. & Hoffman, S. (1985). A reconsideration of the economic consequences of marital dissolution. *Demography*, 22, 485-497.

Duncan, G. & Morgan, J.N., Eds. (1976). Five thousand American families–patterns of economic progress (Vol. 5). Ann Arbor: Institute for social research, University of Michigan.

Eckhardt, K.W. (1968). Deviance, visibility, and legal action: The duty to support. *Social Problems*, 15, 470-477.

Ehrenreich, B. & Piven, F.F. (1984). The feminization of poverty: When the family wage system breaks down. *Dissent*, 31, 162.

Espenshade, T. (1979). The economic consequences of divorce. *Journal of Marriage and Family*, 41, 615-625.

Goldberg, G. (1972). Review of women and welfare: A feminist analysis, by Miller, D.C. *Social Service Review*, 66, 162-167.

Hoffman, S. & Duncan, G. (1988). What are the economic consequences of divorce? *Demography*, 24, 641-645.

Hoffman, S. (1977). Marital instability and the economic status of women, *Demography*, 14, 67-76.

Johnson, W.D. & Minton, M.H. (1982). The economic choice in divorce: Extended or blended family? *Journal of Divorce*, 5, 101-113.

Keith, P. (1985). Financial well-being of older divorced/separated men and women: Findings from a panel study. *Journal of Divorce*, 9, 61-72.

Kitson, G., with Holmes, W. (1991). Portrait of divorce. New York: Guilford Press.

Kitson, G. & Morgan, L. (1990). The multiple consequences of divorce: A decade review. *Journal of Marriage and the Family*, 52, 913-924.

Menard, S. (1991). Longitudinal research. Newberry Park, CA: Sage.

Morgan, L. (1991). After marriage ends: Economic consequences for mid-life women. Newberry Park, CA: Sage.

Okin, S.M. (1991). Economic equality after divorce. *Dissent*, 38, 383-394.

Pett, M.G. (1982). Correlates of children's social adjustment following divorce. *Journal of Divorce*, 5, 25-33.

Schorr, A. & Moen, P. (1979). The single parent and public policy. *Social Policy*, 9, 15-21.

Skolnick, A.S. (1987). The intimate environment: Exploring marriage and the family. Boston: Little, Brown.

Spanier, G. & Thompson, H. (1984). Parting: The aftermath of separation and divorce. Newberry Park, CA: Sage.

Steil, J.M. & Weltman, K. (1991). Marital inequality: The importance of resources, personal attributes, and social norms on career valuing and the allocation of domestic responsibilities. *Sex Roles*, 24, 161-165.

Teachman, J.D. & Polonko, K. (1990). Negotiating divorce outcomes: Can we identify patterns in divorce settlements? *Journal of Marriage and Family*, 52, 129-139.

Teachman, J.D. (1990). Contributions to children by divorced fathers. *Social Problems*, 38, 358-362.

Wattenberg, E. & Reinhardt, H. (1979). Female-headed families: Trends and implications. *Social Work*, 24, 460-467.

Weiss, R.S. (1984). The impact of marital dissolution on income and consumption of single-parent households. *Journal of Marriage and Family*, 46, 115-127.

Weitzman, L. (1985). The divorce revolution. New York: The Free Press.

An Examination of Income Adequacy for Single Women Two Years After Divorce

Celvia Stovall Dixon
Kathryn D. Rettig

SUMMARY. This study reports factors that predict income adequacy for women two years after divorce. The sample for this study was composed of 209 single women responding to the second phase of a longitudinal divorce study in a midwestern state. Results of multiple regression analyses indicated that income adequacy for women after divorce was positively associated with total number of weekly work hours, personal resources of age and education, and perceptions of financial solvency.

Celvia Stovall Dixon, PhD, is Associate Professor, University of Tennessee Agricultural Extension Service, P.O. Box 1071, Knoxville, TN 27901-1071. Kathryn D. Rettig, PhD, is Professor, Department of Family Social Science, 290 McNeal Hall, University of Minnesota, 1985 Buford Avenue, St. Paul, MN 55108.

Data for this paper was provided by the Economic Consequences of Divorce in Minnesota Research Study, Phase II Mail Survey, Kathryn Rettig, Principal Investigator, Lois Yellowthunder, Project Manager. The study was funded by The Bush, St. Paul, and Bigelow Foundations; Ramsey County District Court; The Department of Family Social Science at the University of Minnesota; and The Minnesota Agricultural Experiment Station. The methodologies and interpretations of results in this study are the responsibility of the author and do not represent the views of any of the funding agencies.

[Haworth co-indexing entry note]: "An Examination of Income Adequacy for Single Women Two Years After Divorce." Dixon, Celvia Stovall, and Kathryn D. Rettig. Co-published simultaneously in *Journal of Divorce & Remarriage* (The Haworth Press, Inc.) Vol. 22, No. 1/2, 1994, pp. 55-71; and: *The Economics of Divorce: The Effects on Parents and Children* (ed: Craig A. Everett) The Haworth Press, Inc., 1994, pp. 55-71. Multiple copies of this article/chapter may be purchased from The Haworth Document Delivery Center [1-800-3-HAWORTH; 9:00 a.m. - 5:00 p.m. (EST)].

Divorce is a reality for many Americans as indicated by the more than two-million divorces granted in 1989 (National Center for Health Statistics). Several research studies support the fact that divorce causes tremendous emotional and economic stress for individuals and families (Buehler, Hogan, Robinson, & Levy, 1985; Espenshade, 1979; Tschann, Johnston, Wallerstein, 1980; Weiss, 1976; Weitzman, 1985). The economic stress of divorce is experienced by single women through reduction of income and assets.

Census data have documented low incomes in female-headed households; the data indicated that poverty rates of these households are substantially higher than those in male-headed households (U.S. Census, 1986). Female-headed families constitute about one-half of all poor families; and one-half of these are headed by women who are divorced or separated (Arendell, 1987; Bane, 1986). Nearly half of the female-headed families with children have household incomes below the official U.S. poverty line, and nearly half depend on welfare for a major portion of their income (Garfinkel & McLanahan, 1986).

Many of the previous divorce studies have viewed stress from outsider perspectives where researchers have concluded that subjects experience economic stress. Few studies have concentrated on the perception of economic stress from insiders' perspectives or determined if perceptions of stress are as important in explaining stress recovery as the theoretical stress models have suggested. There also appears to be a gap in the body of divorce research relating individuals' perceptions of their financial situation after a divorce and the relationship of this perception to economic recovery two or more years after a divorce. The family stress conceptual framework developed by Hill (1971) and elaborated by McCubbin and Patterson (1983) and Boss (1988) has been used in the present study to address the issue of economic stress after divorce (Buehler et al., 1980; and Plummer & Koch-Hatten, 1986; Tschann et al., 1989).

The purpose of the present study was to examine how women adapt to the economic stress of the divorce event and to see how these women recover with some level of income adequacy two years later. The divorce process was assumed to have ended with the event of the final decree. The divorce was assumed to have created economic stress due to losses of money income, assets, and human resources. These resource losses would reduce the economic well-being of divorced women. The overall question for this study was: Can income adequacy for women two years after the final divorce decree be predicted by the strains of added work hours, personal resources of education, age, and job seniority, and perceptions of financial solvency?

RELATED LITERATURE

The decade review, which focuses on the multiple consequences of divorce for adults, areas of controversy, and new emphases in studies of divorce, reported that divorce is finally being recognized as one of the most stressful events an individual will face in life, and that the divorce literature is beginning to focus on the nature of divorce adjustment processes (Kitson & Morgan, 1990). The economic adjustment is one of critical importance which needs research attention.

The following studies are summarized using the concepts of the family stress theory framework, including the stressor event, ongoing strains, resources for adaptation, perceptions, and stress-recovery outcome. Boss (1988) defined the stressor event as one that has the potential to cause change because it disturbs the status quo. A strain is the result of a mismatch at the point where pressures occur and the resources and strengths are grounded. Perception is the meaning of the event, and resources are the strengths that are available to cope with the event. Outcome denotes how the process of problem-solving is managed after a problem has been identified (Boss, 1988).

Event

A divorce can have serious consequences for all family members due to the stress caused by reduced money incomes. Researchers agree that individuals experience stress after a divorce because of the immediate changes in family composition, rules, roles, and resources (Ahrons, 1980; Hampton, 1979; Jacobson, 1978). Marital separation and divorce are traumatic experiences for some women and have serious financial implications for custodial mothers (Duncan & Hoffman, 1985; Johnson, 1985; Weiss, 1976, 1984; Weitzman, 1985).

Divorce often leads to a dramatic decline in the level of living for mothers with custody of their children. The incomes of many female-headed households drop below poverty level income after divorce (Espenshade, 1979; Weitzman, 1985). Weiss (1984), in a panel study of income dynamics, found that marital separation and divorce brought drastic changes in both the amounts and sources of household income.

Research also revealed that there appear to be few differences in the kinds of financial difficulties associated with marital disruption for males and females. Both genders report cash flow problems, loss of assets, and loss of the ability to make human capital investments in education for themselves and their children (Rettig, Yellowthunder, Christensen, Dahl, & Ruffin, 1990).

Stressors and Strains

Many women are faced with role strains after a divorce because of the time demands of full-time work and full-time parenting. Single women with custody of children experience intense pressures due to inadequate time and money (Weitzman, 1985). A study of 468 parents working in a Southeastern metropolitan area revealed that only single parents reported strains in assuming their many different roles (Voydanoff & Kelly, 1984). These role strains were experienced in feelings of time shortages, income inadequacy, and job tension.

Divorced women with minor children have higher rates of anxiety and depression than any other marital group (McCubbin, Joy, Cauble, Comeau, Patterson, & Needle, 1980). Wallerstein and Huntington (1983) reported one-third of custodial parents in their study experienced high levels of anxiety after their divorce when they were unable to provide daily living necessities for themselves and their children. Although both men and women experience psychic and physical distress after a divorce, women seem to experience the greater stress attributed to their economic condition.

Resources

The resources, assets, and coping mechanisms utilized after a divorce are important in the adjustment process. Tschann, Johnston and Wallerstein (1989) identified personal and social assets that serve as resources for individual recovery from the emotional and economic losses of divorce. The personal assets were level of education, occupation, age, and pre-separation psychological characteristics. Social assets were social activities, social support, and a new intimate relationship. Mauldin (1991) indicated that there were specific resources and characteristics that explained a woman's ability to move out of poverty after a divorce. The most important variables were current employment, job training, education, and race. Current employment is also dependent upon past employment history, but Mauldin (1991) did not examine job seniority which is an important determinant of income levels. Katz (1991) agreed that the two factors having significant positive effects on the economic well-being of single mothers were education and earnings.

Buehler et al. (1985) reported employment status, educational level, income during marriage, and the number of children as important variables in explaining the economic well-being of single women with children. The number of children and income during marriage were negatively related to the economic well-being of single mothers. Children who require many hours of child care are expensive for working mothers. Women with higher incomes during marriage often face more drastic income reductions after a divorce; they are forced to experience substantial changes in levels of living for themselves and their children (Arendell, 1987; Weitzman, 1985).

Perception of Financial Solvency

Divorce can be perceived differently by individuals experiencing the process. Huddleston and Hawkins (1991) reported that divorce provides relief for some and distress for others, some of whom may experience change in physical and emotional health. Rettig et al. (1990) found men and women have different perceptions of their financial lives after a divorce. Men had higher incomes than women, but were less likely to view their financial situation in a positive manner.

Stress Recovery

Researchers agree that age (Amato & Partridge, 1987; Duffy, 1989; McPhee, 1984), education (Amato, 1987, Duffy, 1989), and money resources (Amato & Partridge, 1987; Linblad-Goldberg & Dukes, 1985) assist in stress recovery, adjustment or well-being after a divorce. A study that focused on the material, personal, family, and social well-being of widows and divorcees found economic well-being of divorced women with dependent children higher if women were young and educated (Amato & Partridge, 1987). Education and income explained 66 percent of the well-being of women in one-parent families (Duffy, 1989). Other factors identified in the literature assisting with stress recovery after a divorce included: personal characteristics, available environmental resources, length of marriage (McPhee, 1984) and financial independence and control (Lindblad-Goldberg & Dukes, 1985).

Divorce recovery, according to the literature review, has many predicting factors. The stress theory model provides an organization for examining these factors. The research question for the study was: Can income adequacy for women two years after a divorce be predicted by (a) strains of total number of weekly work hours; (b) personal resources of age, education, and job seniority; and (c) perceptions of financial solvency? The present study uses insiders' perspectives to determine the relationship between income adequacy two years after a divorce, controlling for the number of hours women work, age, level of education, job seniority, and the perception of financial solvency. The conceptual model for this study is included in Figure 1.

METHODS

Sampling Procedure

The data for this study were obtained from the second phase of a longitudinal divorce research project. The first phase of the project

FIGURE 1. Conceptual Model of Stress Recovery Measured by Income Adequacy.

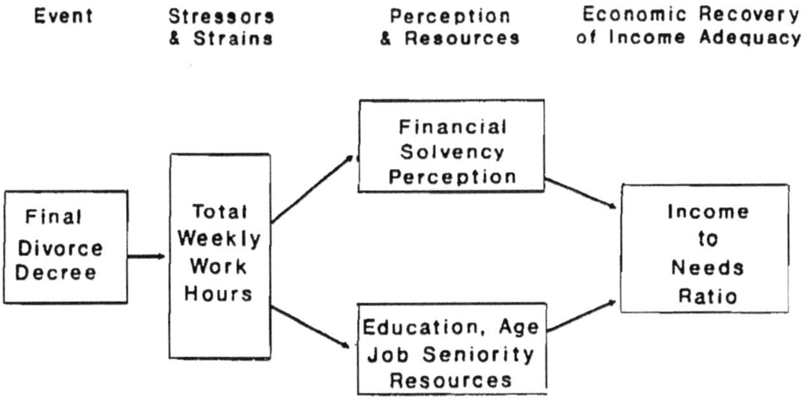

collected data from 1,153 randomly selected court case records in ten counties representing judicial districts in one Midwestern state. The cases represented 19 percent of the 6,117 final divorce decrees in 1986 in which there were minor children. The divorces in the Phase I sample were most often families with one or two children, and the couples had been married an average of 10.6 years. The mean age of the wives was 32 and 35 years of age for the husbands. Phase II of the longitudinal research project focused on collecting information by mail survey from both spouses of the Phase I cases. Updated addresses for both parties were obtained and questionnaires were mailed in October, 1989 to the 909 women and 824 men whose addresses could be located. Completed questionnaires were received from 461 women and 364 men representing 662 cases for a response rate of 57% of the 1153 cases reported in Phase I of the study.

Sample

The second phase of data collection included 322 women who had remained single since the 1986 divorce. Income information was reported by 209 of the single women. The median income for these women was $16,584. Personal median income for the women was $13,800 and child support received was a median of $4,302. The mean age for females in the study sample was 33.5 years. The mean number of years of education was 13.8 years. Respondents reported having been employed on their main job an average of less than 3 years, and worked a mean of 40 hours per week.

MEASURES

Dependent Variable. The outcome measure was stress recovery as indicated by household income adequacy. Household income adequacy was defined as having a household income that would be sufficient to keep the household above the poverty level income. Household income adequacy was measured by using an income-to-needs ratio. The ratio was created from the data by taking the household income for 1988 in the numerator and dividing that amount by the 1988 poverty level income for the household size. Income adequacy was assumed to exist when the ratio of income to income needs was equal to one or higher. A ratio of one indicates the income provides the level of living that the income-need standard requires.

Independent Variables. The predictors of income adequacy two years after a divorce included a strain variable represented by the number of weekly hours women worked outside the home, a perception variable represented by women's perceptions of financial solvency, and resources variables represented by age, education, and job seniority. Education was measured by asking respondents to indicate their highest grade completed. Job seniority was measured by asking respondents to indicate the number of years employed at their main job. The weekly work hours were measured by asking respondents to indicate how many hours per week they worked at their main job and at jobs two and three, if applicable.

Perception of financial solvency was measured with four items which reflected the participants' perceptions of their present financial condition in comparison to their financial condition before divorce, their ability to save money, ability to meet current financial expenses, and to stay out of debt. Respondents answered the items using a 5-point likert scale which ranged from "much worse" (1), "worse" (2), "about the same" (3), "better" (4), to "much better" (5).

The measure of financial solvency was created from the data by adding the scores for the four items and creating a total. Higher scores reflected perceptions of higher financial solvency. The mean score for the Financial Solvency Scale was 11.21 with a Cronbach's alpha of .92 for all women in the Phase II sample.

Data Analyses

The Statistical Package for the Social Sciences (SPSSX) was used to analyze the data (Norusus, 1988). Preliminary data analyses included examination of the frequency distribution of independent variables and correlations to examine relationships among the dependent and predictor variables. Stepwise multiple regression analysis was used to address the research question: Can income adequacy two years after a divorce be predicted by job strain, personal resources and perception of financial solvency?

Standardized regression coefficients were reported because of the differences between and across measures. Standardized regression coefficients treat different units as similar across a normalized distribution (Kerlinger, 1986). Step-wise regression analysis was used to determine the independent variables that were the best predictors of income adequacy. Step-wise regression is useful in model building because it selects the variables in order of their relative strength. This ensures that the elements within the model are the best predictors and therefore exhibits parsimony. Five independent variables were regressed upon the dependent variable of income adequacy. The analytical model for this study is included in Figure 2.

RESULTS

Descriptive Analyses. The descriptive statistics for the dependent variable indicated a mean income-to-needs ratio for the entire sample of 1.89 (median 1.67) with a standard deviation of 1.15. The distribution of income-to-needs ratios for the sample is reported in Table 1. Twenty-four percent ($n = 51$) of the sample had household income-to-need ratios below the poverty level (defined as .99 or

FIGURE 2. Analytical Model of Stress Recovery Measured by Income Adequacy.

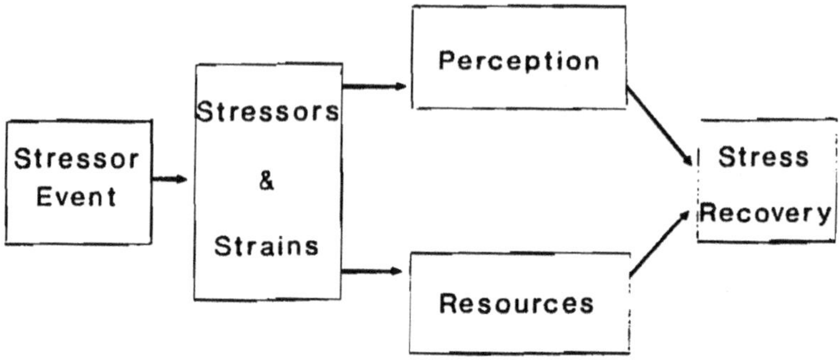

below). Almost 40% (n = 84) had household incomes that were at the poverty level income or slightly above (1.00 - 1.99). Twenty-three percent (n = 49) had household incomes two to 2.99 times above the poverty level and 12.8% (n = 27) had incomes that were three times or greater than the poverty level income. A total of 64% of the sample had incomes less than twice the poverty level. Results from this analysis support other data indicating many single women face poverty after a divorce.

Table 2 summarizes the descriptive statistics for the independent variables. The mean age of single women in the sample was 33.5 years. The mean level of education for the sample was 13.8 years. Most women had been in the labor force less than three years and worked full-time, a mean 32.8 hours per week.

These data suggest that the women in this sample were relatively young, were at least high school educated, and had participated in the work force for a short period of time. The financial solvency variable scores ranged from 4 to 20 and had a mean of 11.06 and a standard deviation of 4.54. This suggested that over half the women in the sample perceived their financial solvency as being about the same prior to their divorce.

Correlation Analyses. Correlations among the variables were examined for multicollinearity which was not a problem since the highest correlation was $r = .53$ p, .001 total work hours and job seniority. Table 3 reports significant positive relationships between

TABLE 1. Income-to-Needs Ratios for Single Women Two Years After Their Divorce.[a]

Value	Percent	Cum %
0.00 - 0.99	24.2	24.2
1.00 - 1.99	39.8	64.0
2.00 - 2.99	23.2	87.0
3.00 - 3.99	7.6	94.8
4.01 & Above	5.2	100.0

[a]n = 209

TABLE 2. Descriptive Statistics for Independent Variables.[a]

Variables	Mean	Median	SD
Total Weekly Work Hours	32.80	40.00	19.24
Age	33.50	33.00	6.75
Education	13.80	13.00	2.07
Job Seniority	2.35	2.00	1.70
Financial Solvency Perception	11.06	10.00	4.54

[a]n = 209

the dependent variable of income adequacy and all of independent variables: total hours worked ($r = .46$ $p < .001$), education ($r = .35$ $p < .001$), financial solvency perception ($r = .19$ $p < .01$), age ($r = .35$ $p < .001$), and job seniority ($r = .32$ $p < .001$).

Multivariate Analyses. The variables in the stepwise regression equation explained 35 percent of the variance in income adequacy. The most important explanatory variable was total weekly work hours ($\beta = .32$, p 0.001), followed by education ($\beta = .29$, $p < 0.001$), financial solvency perception ($\beta = .19$, $p < 0.001$), and age ($\beta = .17$,

TABLE 3. Correlations of Factors Contributing to Recovery of Income Adequacy Two Years After Divorce.[a]

	1	2	3	4	5	6
1. Income Adequacy	1.00					
2. Total Weekly Work Hours	.46***	1.00				
3. Age	.35***	.31***	1.00			
4. Education	.35***	.12	.27***	1.00		
5. Job Seniority	.32***	.53***	.35***	.07	1.00	
6. Financial Solvency Perception	.19**	.12	–.06	–.13	.08	1.00

[a]$\underline{n} = 209$
*$p < 0.05$ **$p < 0.01$ ***$p < 0.001$

$p < 0.01$). Job seniority ($\beta = .06$, $p < 0.40$) did not contribute to reduction of variance in income adequacy, but its inclusion did not detract from the overall variance explained. Table 4 reports the step-wise regression analysis.

DISCUSSION AND IMPLICATIONS

Results of this study provide support for the use of the stress model as an appropriate framework for looking at income adequacy for women two years after a divorce. The regression analysis indicated that the number of hours women work, and their educational level are the best predictors of income adequacy after a divorce. These findings are consistent with other studies in that employed women with more education fare better after a divorce than do women with fewer resources (Buehler et al., 1985; Mauldin, 1991; Tschann, Johnston, & Wallerstein, 1989). Findings reveal that income adequacy is possible two years after divorce for women who work more hours and have a higher educational level. Women must prepare themselves for economic risks such as divorce by seeking more education, preferably a college degree, and having work experience before getting married and while married. Although most people enter marriage with the intent of making it permanent, di-

TABLE 4. Regression Analysis of Factors Contributing to Recovery of Income Adequacy Two Years After Divorce.[a]

	Beta	ADJRSQ	RSQCH	F
Total Work Hours	.32***	.21	.21	56.46***
Education	.29***	.30	.09	44.77***
Financial Solvency Perception	.19***	.33	.03	34.44***
Age	.17**	.35	.03	28.95***
Job Seniority	.06	.35	.00	23.26***

[a]$n = 209$

*$p < .05$ **$p < .01$ ***$p < .001$

vorce statistics indicate that in all likelihood many of these marriages will end.

Correlation and regression analyses revealed that income adequacy was highest for single women who reported higher total work hours. These women are, therefore, likely to face conflict with their time demands. Many have competing goals of time for work and time for their children. Single women are often forced to make decisions to work long hours in order to provide adequate income to meet the needs of their children. Divorce research supports the fact that single women after a divorce are often faced with economic changes that force them into hectic and exhausting work schedules (Weitzman, 1985; Weiss, 1984).

Women with low financial solvency perceptions tended to be older and did not have adequate income to keep their household above poverty level income. When women were asked about their present financial condition, compared to their financial condition before divorce, many women perceived their present financial solvency as being about the same as prior to their divorce. This perception is inconsistent with the objective economic indicators of divorced women in the divorce literature and therefore, raises several questions. Do these women see their financial solvency as about the same because they are recovering and feel better about their situation? Are these women more optimistic because they are employed and have more control over their finances?

Examining single women two years after a divorce could be one limitation of this study. Researchers have indicated that adjustment or recovery after a divorce takes many years (Menaghan & Lieberman, 1986; Weiss, 1984). The women in the sample have been in the work force less than three years and have an educational level of 13.8 years. These women are very likely to be employed in positions making minimum wages, jobs that typically do not provide individuals with incomes above the poverty level.

The educational level and the short length of time that these women have been employed could conceivably be a limitation for the women in this study. In many cases the amount of time on a job and the level of education are strong determinants of income. However, because these women are young, they have many years in which to acquire additional education, seek employment paying higher wages, and to acquire the higher wages that come with seniority.

Another limitation of the study is failure to inquire about assets such as pensions, emergency funds or social security entitlements for survivors benefits, disability, or income from family or possible housemates. Monetary contributions to the household from the above-mentioned sources could affect perceptions of financial solvency after a divorce.

The consistency of findings in this study along with other studies suggest the need to educate women on the importance of making personal investments in themselves prior to and during marriage. Family educators, counselors, therapists, and financial planners must become aware of educational programming needs of divorced women. Education for these women should include knowledge of the consequences of divorce without an education and work experience. Women must learn to assume an active role in financial affairs during marriage. Skills in this area are manadatory for survival after a divorce.

Economic well-being of women with children after a divorce continues to be a concern on both the state and national level. This study revealed that women who worked longer hours reported higher income adequacy. Longer work hours mean fewer hours for single women to spend with their children. Findings from this study indicate a need for family policies that financially protect families with children after a divorce. Single mothers should not have to sacrifice income for time to spend with children. Parents must become aware of the importance of socializing children at an early age to become not only capable, productive members in society but to become self-sufficient adults capable of supporting themselves whether married or not.

REFERENCES

Ahrons, C. (1980). Divorce: A crisis of family transition and change. *Family Relations, 29*, 533-540.

Amato, P., & Partridge, S. (1987). Widows and divorcees with dependent children: Material, personal, family social well-being. *Family Relations, 36*, 316-320.

Arendell, T. (1987). Women and the economics of divorce in the contemporary United States. *Signs, 13*, 121-135.

Bane, M. J. (1986). Household Composition and Poverty. in Danziger, S. and Weinberg, D. (Eds.), *Fighting Poverty*, Massachusetts: Harvard Press, pp. 209-231.

Boss, P. (1988). *Family Stress Management*. California: Sage.

Buehler, C., Hogan, M. J., Robinson, B., & Levy, R. J. (1985). The parental divorce transition: Divorce-related stressors and well-being, *Journal of Divorce*, *9*, 61-80.

Buehler, C., & Langenbrunner, M. (1987). Divorce-related stressors: occurrence, disruptiveness and area of life change, *Journal of Divorce*, *11*, 25-50.

Caldwell, R. A., Bloom, B. A., & Hodges, W. F. (1983). Sex differences in separation and divorce: A longitudinal perspective, *Issues in Mental Health Nursing*, *5*, 103-120.

Corcoran, M., Duncan, G. J., & Hill, M. S. (1984). The economic fortunes of women and children: Lessons from the panel study of income dynamics. *Signs*, *10*, 232-248.

Duffy, M. (1989). Mental well-being of women in one-parent families, *Journal of Divorce*, *13*, 45-57.

Duncan, G. J., & Hoffman, S. D. (1985). A reconsideration of the economic consequences of marital disruption. *Demography*, *22*, 485-498.

Espenshade, T. J. (1979). The economic consequences of divorce. *Journal of Marriage and the Family*, *41*, 615-625.

Garfinkel, I., & McLanahan, S. (1986). *Single Mothers and Their Children*. Washington DC: Urban Institute.

Hampton, R. L. (1979). Marital disruption: Some social and economic consequences. in J. N. Morgan (Ed.), *Five Thousand American Families*, Vol. 3, Ann Arbor, MI: Institute for Social Research, pp. 163-187.

Hill, R. (1971). *Families under stress*. Westport, CT: Greenwood.

Huddleston, R. J., & Hawkins, L. (1991). A comparison of physical and emotional health after divorce in a Canadian and United States' sample. *Journal of Divorce*, *15*, 193-207.

Jacobson, G. F. (1978). Impact of marital separation on children: I. P-C separation and child adjustment. *Journal of Divorce*, *1*, 341-360.

Johnson, C. L. (1985). Single mothers following separation and divorce: Making it on your own, *Family Relations*, *35*, 189-197.

Katz, R. (1991). Marital status and well-being: A comparison of widowed, divorced, and married mothers in Israel, *Journal of Divorce*, *14*, 203-218.

Kerlinger, F. (1986). *Foundations of Behavioral Research*. New York: Holt, Rinehart and Winston, Inc.

Kitson, G. C., & Morgan, L. A. (1990). The Multiple consequences of divorce: A decade review. *Journal of Marriage and the Family*, *52*, 913-922.

Lindblad-Goldberg, M., & Dukes, J. (1985). Social support in black, low income, single-parent families. *American Journal of Orthopsychiatry*, *55*, 42-58.

Mauldin, T. A. (1991). Economic consequences of divorce or separation among women in poverty, *Journal of Divorce*, *14*, 163-177.

McCubbin, H., Joy, C., Couble, A., Comeau, J., Patterson, J., & Needle, R.

(1980). Family stress and coping: A decade of review. *Journal of Marriage and the Family, 42*, 855-71.

McCubbin, H., & Patterson, J. (1983). The family stress process: The double ABCX model of family adjustment and adaptation. In H. McCubbin, M. Sussman, & J. Patterson (Eds.). *Advances and developments in family stress theory and research*. New York: The Haworth Press, Inc.

McLanahan, S., Wedemeyer, N., & Adelberg, T. (1981). Network, structure, social support and psychological well-being in the single parent family. *Journal of Marriage and the Family, 43*, 601-612.

McPhee, T. (1984). Ambiguity and change in post-divorce families. *Journal of Divorce, 8*, 1-16.

National Center for Health Statistics (1989). Births, marriages, divorces, and deaths for April 1989, *Monthly Vital Statistics, 38*, August 2.

Norusus, M. (1988). *SPSSX* : Chicago: SPSS Inc.

Pett, M. A., & Vaughan-Cole, B. (1986). The impact of income issues and social status on post-divorce adjustment of custodial parents. *Family Relations, 35*, 103-112.

Plummer, L. P., & Koch-Hatten, P. (1986). Family stress and adjustment to divorce, *Family Relations, 35*, 523-529.

Rettig, K. D., Yellowthunder, L., Dahl, C. M., Christensen, D. H., & Ruffin, W. J. (1990). Economic consequences of divorce in Minnesota: Phase II research report. St. Paul, MN: Department of Family Social Science, University of Minnesota.

Tschann, J. M., Johnson, J. R., & Wallerstein, J. S. (1989). Resources, stresses, and attachment as predictors of adult adjustment after a divorce: A longitudinal study. *Journal of Marriage and the Family, 51*, 1033-1046.

U.S. Bureau of the Census (1986). Households, families, marital status, and living arrangements, series p-23, No. 370 current population reports, March 1986. Washington, DC: U.S. Government printing office.

Voydanoff, P., & Kelly, R. (1984). Determinants of work-related family problems among employed parents. *Journal of Marriage and the Family, 46*, 881-892.

Wallerstein, J. S. & Huntington, D. S. (1983). Bread and roses: Non-financial issues related to fathers' economic support of their children following divorce. In J. Cassetty (Ed.), *The Parental Child-Support Obligation*. Lexington, MA: Lexington Books, pp. 135-155.

Wallerstein, J., & Kelly, J. B. (1980). *Surviving the breakup: How children and parents cope with divorce*. New York: Basic Books.

Weiss, R. (1976). The emotional impact of marital separation. *Journal of Social Issues, 32*, 135-145.

Weiss, R. S. (1984). The impact of marital dissolution on income and consumption in single-parent households. *Journal of Marriage and the Family, 46*, 115-127.

Weitzman, L. J. (1985). *The divorce revolution*. New York: The Free Press.

A Comparison of Single and Married Working Parents' Agency and Desire for Money

Sara R. Mahler

SUMMARY. Much research has been devoted to work-family relationships, but almost none has focused on single working parents. The present research compared a volunteer sample of single and married working parents of both sexes. Solo parents were found to engage in more agentic behavior than their married counterparts, but were only marginally more agentic in their self-concept. However, unlike married parents, agentic behavior had no relationship with well-being. Although analysis of variance showed they valued extrinsic rewards from work more than married parents, covariance analysis revealed that this was associated with their relative economic deprivation.

Single working parents are a significant proportion of all families with children, yet little is known about how they manage their dual roles as worker and parent. In the United States, single parent families represent 25% of all family groups with children under age 18 (Shellinberger, 1993), and their labor force participation rates are

---

Sara R. Mahler, PhD, is on the faculty of Hartwick College, Oneonta, NY 13820.

This article is based on Dr. Mahler's doctoral dissertation submitted to the City University of New York. The author thanks Professor Lawrence Podell for his helpful comments on an earlier draft of this paper.

[Haworth co-indexing entry note]: "A Comparison of Single and Married Working Parents' Agency and Desire for Money." Mahler, Sara R. Co-published simultaneously in *Journal of Divorce & Remarriage* (The Haworth Press, Inc.) Vol. 22, No. 1/2, 1994, pp. 73-86; and: *The Economics of Divorce: The Effects on Parents and Children* (ed: Craig A. Everett) The Haworth Press, Inc., 1994, pp. 73-86. Multiple copies of this article/chapter may be purchased from The Haworth Document Delivery Center [1-800-3-HAWORTH; 9:00 a.m. - 5:00 p.m. (EST)].

generally higher than that of married parents. According to U.S. Department of Labor figures (1987), labor force participation rates were 60.9% for single mothers and 82% for single fathers, compared to 56.7% and 89.5% for married mothers and fathers respectively.

Single parenthood is a transitional state, generally lasting a few years. Projections made by Norton and Glick, assuming no change in rates of marital dissolution or premarital birth, indicate that nearly 60% of all children born in 1984 may be expected to spend a year or longer in a one-parent family before reaching age 18 (Norton & Glick, 1986, pp. 15-16). Therefore, a substantially greater portion of the working population will be affected by single-parenthood over the next two decades than cross-sectional survey data indicates.

Although a large body of single-parent literature exists in various disciplines, it concentrates on the effects of absence of a parent on the children, public policy issues surrounding child welfare payments, and economic deprivations experienced by single mothers (Ross & Sawhill, 1976; Epstein, 1979; Pett & Vaughan-Cole, 1986). There is little about how they are able to manage their dual roles of sole worker and sole parent, and, with few exceptions (Quinn & Staines, 1978; Pleck, 1979; Best, 1980; Paloma, Pendelton & Garland, 1982; Anderson-Kulman & Paludi, 1986; Burden, 1986), single parents have not been placed within a general working-parent framework.

In two-parent families, the roles of worker and parent are either divided or shared. These roles were often divided between the father, as the Provider, and the mother, as the Nurturer. The Provider role was the socially sanctioned male sex role, and believed to require agentic characteristics; that is, a cognitive focus on solving problems and obtaining goals. The Nurturer role was the socially sanctioned female role, believed to require communal behavior; an affective concern for group harmony and the welfare of others (Bakan, 1966). Within two-paycheck families, these roles are usually shared rather than divided, each parent taking some portion of both roles.

Single working parents, however, have sole responsibility for both roles. Although they may have assistance from relatives, live in multi-family households, or receive regular child-support payments, full responsibility generally remains with them. The organization of society for the two-parent family therefore creates extreme demands on the solo parent's time and energy, as well as additional economic burdens.

Evidence has accumulated indicating that psychological characteristics of adults are affected by occupational experiences (Fogarty, Rapoport & Rapoport, 1971; Kohn & Schooler, 1973; Hoffman & Fidell, 1979), and parenthood (Abrahams, Feldman & Nash, 1978; Wilensky, 1981). Solitary parents were found to have a higher incidence of depression (Pearlin & Johnson, 1977), and lower sense of control over their lives than married people (Weiss, 1976). However, a national survey reported less work-family conflict for single mothers (Pleck, 1979), and, although Burden (1986) found higher role strain for single parents, Anderson-Kulman and Paludi (1986) found no differences between single and married parents.

Research reviews of responses to marital dissolution show that traditional sex role attitudes during marriage are negatively related to adjustment (Pledge, 1992), and women with non-traditional sex role attitudes have fewer post-divorce adjustment problems (Hanson & Spanier, 1983). Working mothers reported themselves more agentic than housewives (Hoffman & Fidell, 1979), and single parents were found to use more instrumental than expressive behaviors regardless of sex (Rasmussen, 1975). Single working mothers maintained more intra-family organization than married mothers (Anderson-Kulman & Paludi, 1986), indicative of an agentic orientation.

As family role, agency focuses on establishing desired relationships to goal objects, and is analogous to the task specialist of small groups (Parsons & Bales, 1955). By actively attempting to change the environment, agentic behaviors may be capable of restructuring situational demands under conditions of heavy time and energy constraints with pressures to perform. This is characteristic of the working single parent's situation. However, the extent of congruence between agentic behavior and self-concept has been a subject of debate in the literature. Consensus appears to be that, if specific situations are perceived to demand behavior not congruent with the individual's self-concept, and conformity to these demands is considered important, individuals may behave in a manner not congruent with their self-concepts (Lenny, 1979; Risman, 1983).

Single parent families have lower incomes than intact families. This is especially true of female headed families, whose median income was only 38% of that of married couple families with children in 1985 (U.S. Bureau of the Census, 1986). Many poor female-headed families were not poor prior to marital dissolution (Kriesberg, 1970). Data from a national survey revealed that a sharp drop in income occurs in the first year following marital dissolution, followed by a marked rise in the second and third years, which is accompanied by a high level of employment related movement (McLanahan, 1983).

Divorced and separated women were almost three times as likely to worry about money all or most of the time as opposed to married women (Weiss, 1976). Single mothers were found less likely to be willing to forgo pay for more time off, and also more likely to want more work time for more money than men (Quinn & Staines, 1978; Best, 1980). This, despite child care difficulties, may be indicative of their relatively low incomes.

The purpose of this research was to examine possible differences between single and married working parents with respect to agentic orientation and behavior, and work attachments. Specifically, it was anticipated that levels of agency would be higher among single parents than their married counterparts, and that agentic behavior, rather than self-concept, would be more strongly associated with marital status and well-being. A second focus was to examine the extent that value for extrinsic rewards, expected to be greater for solo parents, is related to their generally lower incomes.

METHOD

Subjects and Procedure

A twelve page questionnaire was distributed to volunteers who were obtained from a variety of sources in a suburb of New York City: Day care centers (39%), PTA groups (8%), and through personal and evening student contacts (27%). In order to increase the proportion of single parents, additional subjects were solicited from single parent organizations (14%). To increase the number of fathers, a classified ad was placed in an area newspaper (12%). This multi-pronged approach was intended to obtain a heterogeneous group, and in particular, to avoid the clinical population bias often found in single parent samples that were obtained through community service agencies. Widowed and never-married custodial parents were excluded in order to avoid confounding reason for single parenthood with the hypothesized relationships. These sub-groups have sometimes demonstrated different characteristics from divorced and separated parents.

The final sample consisted of 227 working parents with children under 18 living at home: 58 divorced or separated mothers, 95 married mothers, 21 divorced or separated fathers, and 53 married fathers. The age of the participants ranged from 22 to 57, with a mean of 36.6. The average number of children living at home was 1.57. Total family income ranged from under \$10,000 to over \$100,000, with 58.3% reporting income of \$35,000 or higher, and 57.7% of the respondents were in managerial or professional positions.

Table 1 presents means and standard deviations on all of the variables for the four sub-samples. These show that the single parent sample was less affluent, less educated, held lower level jobs and also had somewhat older children than the married parents. This reflects differences found between single and married parents in the population-at-large, although at a generally higher socioeconomic level.

Measures

Agentic self-concept was measured by the Masculinity and Masculinity/Femininity subscales of the Personal Attributes Questionnaire (Spence, Helmreich & Stapp, 1974), a self-report instrument consisting of trait descriptions, each set up on a bipolar scale containing eight items. The Masculinity scale contains characteristics considered socially desirable for both sexes but that men are believed to possess to a greater degree than females (e.g., independence). The Masculinity/Femininity scale consists of traits whose social desirability varies in the two sexes (e.g., dominance is considered desirable in males, but its opposite, submissiveness, desirable in females), and is scored in the masculine direction. Coeffi-

TABLE 1. Means and Standard Deviations

Mothers				
	Single (n = 58)		Married (n = 95)	
	X	SD	X	SD
Family income	5.5	2.4	10.3	2.6
Age	36.6	6.3	35.7	6.2
Type of work[a]	3.8	2.4	2.9	1.8
Education[b]	3.5	1.5	4.1	1.6
Eldest child[c]	2.1	.8	1.7	.85
M	2.6	.6	2.5	.55
M/F	1.9	.55	1.7	.5
Task behavior	2.3	.5	2.1	.5
Value extrinsic	15.3	4.7	12.2	4.4
Well-being	3.0	.6	3.2	.7

Fathers				
	Single (n = 21)		Married (n = 53)	
	X	SD	X	SD
Family income	7.9	3.0	9.8	2.7
Age	40.0	6.2	37.0	6.8
Type of work[a]	4.6	3.6	2.8	2.7
Education[b]	3.3	1.6	4.2	1.7
Eldest child[c]	2.5	.7	1.8	.9
M	2.7	.6	2.7	.5
M/F	2.0	.6	2.0	.5
Task behavior	2.2	.4	2.0	.5
Value extrinsic	17.6	5.3	16.6	4.6
Well-being	3.1	.9	3.2	.6

a the lower the number, the higher the level job
b From 1 = some high school to 6 = graduate degree
c 1 = 5 or younger, 2 = 6 to 12, 3 = 13 to 18

cient alpha has been reported to range from .85 to .67 for M, and from .78 to .53 for M/F (Helmreich, Spence & Wilhelm, 1981; Spence & Helmreich, 1978), considered acceptable for a relatively short instrument. Test-retest reliability at 2 1/2 weeks was .87 and .90 for men, on M and M/F respectively (Mahler, 1984).

Agentic behavior was measured by the Task Orientation subscale of the Task-Relationship orientation Day-to-Day Behavior Scale, in which the respondent is asked to indicate the extent to which the behavioral descriptions given are characteristic of them, using a four-point Likert-type format. This scale was developed by first amassing a large item pool from interviews with working parents and literature search. Then, a panel of 12 judges reduced the number of items by categorizing them according to type of orientation and social desirability. Items which had majority agreement were retained, and subjected to orthogonal factor analysis with the main sample. Items of the subscale used in this study are: "Keep working on a problem until it's solved." "Won't hesitate to do something unusual to solve a problem if I believe it will work." "Look ahead, in order to avoid a potential crisis." "Do things myself without help, as much as possible." "Periodically reassess my areas of strength and areas needing improvement." This five-item scale had a coefficient alpha of .62, acceptable for a scale of this length, and showed correlations with the M and M/F scales of the PAQ of .47 and .27, respectively.

Work attachments were measured by a nine item scale, based on Locke's (1976) three categories of intrinsic, extrinsic and contextual job characteristics. The items were adapted from the Quality of Employment Survey Importance of Job Characteristics Scale (Quinn & Staines, 1978). In order to minimize the possibility of rating all job characteristics as "important," a ranking procedure was used, with each category containing an equal number of items. Lefkowitz, Somers and Weinberg (1984) have pointed out that each category within the ranking must contain an equal number of items, so that the probability of an item from any one category being ranked first is equal. The scores were coded and summed for each dimension so that the more important items were given higher numbers.

Well-being was measured by two items used in the Quality of

Employment Survey (Quinn & Staines, 1978): "Taking all things together, how would you say things are these days. Would you say you're very happy, pretty happy, or not too happy these days?" and "In general, how satisfying do you find the way you're spending your life these days? Would you call it completely satisfying, pretty satisfying, or not very satisfying?" Internal consistency of the two-item measure was .72.

Occupation was classified according to the U.S. Bureau of the Census thirteen category system (1980). Family income asked for total family income, in a fifteen category response format that ranged from under $5000 to $100,000 or more.

Data Analysis

Multivariate and univariate analysis of variance and covariance were the primary analytic techniques. Multivariate analysis was used because repeated univariate analysis of variance ignores inter-correlations among the dependent variables, and thus would not have provided as strict a test of differences across means. The classic regression approach, which partitions individual effects by adjusting for *all* other effects, was used in all of the analyses because cell sizes were unequal, and this method provides the most rigorous test for non-orthogonal designs. The usual sequential model gives priority to effects by the sequence in which they are entered, thereby possibly yielding different results based on the ordering of the independent variables in the equation.

RESULTS

Table 2 presents the results of a 2 × 2 MANCOVA of marital status and sex on the three measures of agency, and includes an analysis of the univariate effects of each dependent variable. The covariates were educational level, occupational classification, age, age of eldest child and family income. Regression analysis for the covariates revealed that only family income on the two self-concept

TABLE 2. Results of Multivariate Analysis of Covariance on Agency

	Multivariate		Univariate			
				M	M/F	Behavior
	df	F	df	F	F	F
Covariates	15,591	1.39	5,197	3.05*	1.5	1.5
Status	3.195	4.69**	1,197	3.6	3.34	13.06***
Sex	3,195	1.96	1,197	2.41	2.87	.43
Status X sex	3,195	1.1	1,197	.49	3.15	.2

Means Adjusted for the Five Covariates

	Mothers		Fathers	
	Single	Married	Single	Married
M	2.7	2.41	2.82	2.65
M/F	1.96	1.58	2.06	1.92
Task behavior	2.41	1.97	2.30	1.96

*p < .05
**p < .01
***p < .001

measures was significant (M: beta = .17, p < .05; MF: beta = .18, p < .05), indicating that agentic self-concept was somewhat enhanced by successful providing.

The only significant multivariate effect was for marital status, confirming the hypothesis that single parents are higher in agency than married parents. Furthermore, examination of the univariate effects show that the significant effect was confined to the behavioral measure ($F_{1,197}$ = 13.06; p < .001). The two self-concept measures only approached significance in the hypothesized direction (M: $F_{1,197}$ = 3.6, p = .059; MF: $F_{1,197}$ = 3.34, p = .069), supporting the prediction of stronger association with the behavioral measure.

Regression analysis was performed on single and married parents separately to analyze the effects of the three measures of agency on well-being. Results were significant for the married parents only (multiple R = .25, p = .025, n = 144 versus R = .22, p = .30, n = 75 for single parents). The behavioral measure made the sole significant contribution (beta = .26, p < .01), again confirming the relative importance of behavior over self-concept.

Table 3 compares the results of analysis of variance with analysis of covariance of value for extrinsic rewards. A 2 × 2 ANOVA yielded significant main effects for both marital status and sex. Single parents valued extrinsic rewards more than married parents (x = 15.91 and 13.79, respectively), and men more than women (x = 16.87 and 13.3, respectively). However, when family income was introduced as covariate, the main effect for marital status disappeared, indicating that the difference in work attachments between single and married parents results from their income differences. Regression analysis for the covariate showed that as income decreased, value for extrinsic rewards increased (beta = −.20, p < .01).

DISCUSSION

Single parents were found to be more agentic in their self-reported behavior, but agentic self-concept was only marginally higher than married parents'. This provides additional evidence for the proposition that congruence between self-concept and enacted

TABLE 3. Comparison of ANOVA and ANCOVA on Value for Extrinsic Rewards.

	ANOVA (df = 1,204)		ANCOVA (df = 1,197)	
	MS	F	MS	F
Family income			169.85	8.18**
Status	158.77	7.48**	14.19	.68
Sex	415.44	19.57***	418.79	20.17***
Status X sex	39.95	1.88	18.14	.87

**p < .01
***p < .001

behavior is moderated by situational demands. The findings indicate that behavioral measures may have more utility for uncovering crucial associations, and it is suggested that future research efforts make more use of behavioral reports, in addition to and/or in place of the more commonly used attitudinal measures.

Well-being was modestly associated with agency for the married parents, but not for the single parents. This lack of significant results for the single parents echoes Pleck's (1979) finding with respect to work-family interference and well-being, where solo parents, unlike the rest of the parent sample, showed no correlation between the two measures. Pleck speculated that the more vulnerable position of single parents makes them more strongly affected by other more obvious factors, so that the effect of work-family interference is trivial by comparison. In the present study, the lack of effects for agency may also indicate that such factors as loneliness, depleted energy, role overload and time pressures, economic pressures and feelings of failure and/or inadequacy overshadow any gains from an agentic orientation.

Solo parents' higher value for the extrinsic rewards from work appears to be based on their position of relative economic deprivation, and possibly also insecurity with the Provider role and lack of a partner to act as backup. Similar analyses were performed on this sample for intrinsic rewards and convenience facets. The only differences found were traditional differences between mothers and fathers on the value for convenience facets, with married mothers valuing these the most. Consequently, the tentative conclusion is that there are no inherent differences in work attachments between the two family structures other than those resulting from perceived or actual economic need.

Limitations

The respondents were better educated and more affluent than the working parent population at large, and had fewer children per family. These factors may have contributed to their ability and willingness to complete a lengthy questionnaire. It is also a virtually all-White sample, precluding examination of possible racial and/or ethnic effects.

The conceptual framework posits a causal sequence but the research design was correlational, which does not permit inferences of causality. It is possible that there are certain types of individuals who are predisposed to become single parents, and not that the state of single parenthood causes higher or lower levels of a characteristic. It is possible that both are correct. There may be qualities and/or circumstances that increase an individual's likelihood of becoming a single parent, and, once having become a single parent, that situation adds its impact to the individual's characteristics.

Implications for Practice

Employing organizations have begun to recognize the needs of the two-paycheck family by providing company assistance with child care needs, cafeteria benefit plans, and flexible work schedules. The needs of single parents fit easily within this framework. Assistance with child care may include company sponsored day care centers, referral services, or monetary allowances.

Company sponsored centers benefit those whose children fall within the limited age groups served, generally 18 months to 5 years, leaving out large numbers of young school age children and infants. Single parents, pressed for time–as well as two-paycheck parents–may find it difficult to coordinate the day care needs of both their pre-school and school age children unless both can be attended to in the same place. This argues for assistance towards neighborhood centers, where schoolchildren can join their younger siblings, or in-home day care.

The choice can be given to the parent via a flexible benefit plan, which could include child care allowances and additional personal time for child care emergencies. Exigencies of family life, such as children's illness, occasionally require parental attention during work time. Flexible hours or alternative schedules, including "flexiplace," where employees do part of their work at home, allow parents to work during those hours when child care is available, and may make the difference between keeping a productive employee or having to recruit and train a new one.

REFERENCES

Abrahams, B., Feldman, S. & Nash, S. C. (1978). Sex-role self-concept and sex-role attitudes: Enduring personality characteristics or adaptations to changing life situations? *Developmental Psychology, 14*, 393-400.

Anderson-Kulman, R. E. & Paludi, M. A. (1986). Working mothers and the family context: Predicting positive coping. *Journal of Vocational Behavior, 28*, 241-253.

Bakan, D. (1966). *The duality of human existence.* Boston: Beacon.

Best, F. (1980). *Exchanging earnings for leisure: Findings of an exploratory national study on work time preferences* (R & D Monograph #79). Washington, D.C. Employment and Training Administration, U.S. Department of Labor.

Burden, D. S. (1986). Single parents and the work setting: The impact of multiple job and homelife responsibilities. *Family Relations, 35*, 45-52.

Epstein, M. F. (1979). Children living in one-parent families. *Family Economics Review*, Winter, 21-23.

Fogarty, M. P., Rapoport, R. & Rapoport, R. N. (1971). *Sex, career and family.* Beverly Hills: Sage.

Hanson, L. & Spanier, B. (1983). Family development and adjustment to marital separation. *Sociology & Social Research, 68*(1), 19-48.

Helmreich, R. L., Spence, J. T. & Wilhelm, J. A. (1981). A psychometric analysis of the Personal Attributes Questionnaire. *Sex Roles, 7*, 1097-1107.

Hoffman, D. M. & Fidell, L. S. (1979). Characteristics of androgynous, undifferentiated, masculine and feminine middle-class women. *Sex Roles, 5*, 765-781.

Kohn, M. L. & Schooler, C. (1973). Occupational experience and psychological functioning: An assessment of reciprocal effects. *American Sociological Review, 38*, 97-118.

Kriesberg, L. (1970). *Mothers in poverty: A study of fatherless families.* Chicago: Aldine.

Lefkowitz, J., Somers, M. & Weinberg, K. (1984). The role of need level and/or need salience as moderators of the relationship between need satisfaction and work alienation and involvement. *Journal of Vocational Behavior, 24*, 142-158.

Lenny, E. (1979). Androgyny: Some audacious assertions toward its coming of age. *Sex Roles, 5*, 703-719.

Locke, E. A. (1976). The nature and causes of job satisfaction. In M. D. Dunnette (Ed.), *Handbook of industrial and organizational psychology.* Chicago: Rand-McNally, 1297-1351.

Mahler, S. R. (1984). Test-retest reliability of the Personal Attributes Questionnaire. Unpublished raw data.

McLanahan, S. S. (1983). Family structure and stress: A longitudinal comparison of two-parent and female headed families. *Journal of Marriage and the Family, 45*, 349-357.

Norton, A. J. & Glick, P. C. (1986). One parent families: A social and economic profile. *Family Relations, 35*, 9-18.

Parsons, T. & Bales, R. F. (1955). *Family, socialization and interaction process.* Glencoe, Ill.: Free Press.

Pearlin, L. I. & Johnson, J. S. (1977). Marital status, life strains and depression. *American Sociological Review, 42*, 704-715.

Pett, M. A. & Vaughan-Cole, B. 1986. The impact of income issues and social status on post-divorce adjustment of single parents. *Family Relations, 35*, 103-112.

Pleck, J. H. (1979). *Work-family conflict: A national assessment*. Washington, DC: U.S. Dept. of Labor.

Pledge, D. S. (1992). Marital separation/divorce: A review of individual responses to a major life stressor. *Journal of Divorce & Remarriage, 17*(3/4), 151-182.

Poloma, M. M., Pendleton, B. F. & Garland, T. N. (1982). Reconsidering the dual-career marriage. In J. Aldous (Ed.), *Two paychecks: Life in dual career families*. Beverly Hills: Sage, 173-192.

Quinn, R. P. & Staines, G. L. (1977). *The 1977 Quality of Employment Survey*. Ann Arbor, Mich.: SRC, University of Michigan.

Rasmussen, D. P. (1974). *Sex-role differentiation in single-parent families*. Doctoral Dissertation, University of Wisconsin-Madison.

Risman, B. J. (1983). *Necessity and the invention of mothering: A test of individual versus structural explanations of gender roles*. Doctoral Dissertation, University of Washington.

Ross, H. L. & Sawhill, I. V. (1975). *Time of transition: The growth of families headed by women*. Washington, DC: The Urban Institute.

Shellinberger, S. (1993). So much talk, so little action. *Wall Street Journal*. June 13, R2, 4, 6.

Spence, J. T. & Helmreich, R. L. (1978). *Masculinity and femininity: Their psychological dimensions, correlates and antecedents*. Austin, TX: University of Texas.

Spence, J. T., Helmreich, R. L. & Stapp, J. (1974). The PAQ: A measure of sex-role stereotypes and masculinity and femininity. *JSAS catalogue of selected documents in psychology, 4*, 43.

U.S. Bureau of the Census. (1980). Alphabetical index of industries and occupations. *1980 Census of the Population*, Washington, DC: Government Printing Office.

U.S. Bureau of the Census (1986). Marital status and living arrangements, March, 1985. *Current Population Reports (Series P-20)*, Washington, DC: Government Printing Office.

U.S. Department of Labor, Bureau of Labor Statistics (1987). Families at work: The jobs and the pay. *Special Labor Force Report (Bulletin #2209)*, Washington, DC: Government Printing Office.

Weiss, R. S. (1976). *A preliminary examination of the potential contributions of quality of life data to an understanding of single parenting*. Washington, DC: U.S. Department of Commerce, National Technical Information Service.

Wilensky, H. L. (1981). Family life cycle, work and the quality of life: Reflections on the roots of happiness, despair and indifference in modern society. In B. Gardell & G. Johansson (Eds.). *Working life: A social science contribution to work reform*. New York: Wiley, pp. 235-266.

The Impact of Wives' Employment on Attitude Toward Divorce

Vijaya Krishnan

SUMMARY. Previous studies indicated a relationship between wives' employment and marital instability. Although there are several notable exceptions, the theoretically predicted positive link between wives' employment and marital instability/divorce remains popular. This paper explores the extent to which wives' employment affects their attitudes toward divorce, once religious and other sociodemographic variables are statistically controlled. The data are taken from the 1983-1984 Canadian Fertility Survey of 5,315 women aged 18 to 49.

The overall effect of wives' employment on divorce attitude is substantial, indicating that employed women are more likely to favour marriage as a permanent union. Many popular notions about the influence of demographic and socioeconomic factors such as age, age at marriage, children and occupational prestige on divorce attitude, are not supported by this research. At the same time, religious factors significantly predict divorce attitudes. The results suggest that the less educated, employed, highly religious and heterogeneous are more likely to agree that marriage is a permanent union which should only be broken for very serious reasons.

Vijaya Krishnan, PhD, is with Child Welfare Services, Alberta Family and Social Services, Edmonton, Canada.

This article is a revised version of a paper presented at the Canadian Sociology and Anthropology Association Meetings, Queen's University, Kingston, Ontario, Canada, June 1-4, 1991. The author is grateful to Dr. Karol J. Krotki, Coordinator of the Canadian Fertility Study, for permission to analyze the Canadian Fertility Survey data.

[Haworth co-indexing entry note]: "The Impact of Wives' Employment on Attitude Toward Divorce." Krishnan, Vijaya. Co-published simultaneously in *Journal of Divorce & Remarriage* (The Haworth Press, Inc.) Vol. 22, No. 1/2, 1994, pp. 87-101; and: *The Economics of Divorce: The Effects on Parents and Children* (ed: Craig A. Everett) The Haworth Press, Inc., 1994, pp. 87-101. Multiple copies of this article/chapter may be purchased from The Haworth Document Delivery Center [1-800-3-HAWORTH; 9:00 a.m. - 5:00 p.m. (EST)].

Since 1960 there have been dramatic changes in the demography of the Canadian family. Perhaps the two most striking changes have been in the dramatic increase in the labour force participation rates of married women and in the divorce rate. In 1986, 56.1 percent of all married women worked outside the home, up from 42.8 percent in 1976 (Townson, 1987). Of the marital dissolutions that occurred in 1965, only 11 percent were due to divorce whereas in 1985, this percentage moved up to the figure of 42, representing a 35 percent increase in 20 years. In this context, we are inclined to believe the existence of a positive link between wife's labour force participation and marital instability.

In spite of the extensive research in wives' employment and marital instability, most of the studies have been confined to the United States. A primary objective of this paper is to examine the relationship of wives' employment to attitude toward divorce among women in Canada. A second goal is to attempt to assess the importance of religious factors in explaining such attitudes. The basic question attempted is: net of other sociodemographic correlates, is there an effect of the employment status of married women on attitude toward divorce? To answer this question, the data gathered on a national probability sample of Canadian women were examined employing a multivariate approach.

The following section provides a brief review of the empirical literature linking the employment of wives to marital instability/divorce. The hypotheses are presented, drawing on past research. In the next section, the data set and the method employed in the study are described. The next section focuses on the results. The final section summarizes the results of the paper and comments on them in relation to results presented in studies of marital instability. This section also speculates on the implications of the results for the Canadian family as well as for future research on the subject.

WIVES' EMPLOYMENT AND MARITAL INSTABILITY

Current interest in the relationship between the employment of wives and marital instability/divorce can be traced back to Thwing and Thwing's (1986) study. Since that time a number of studies have established a positive link between marital instability and employment of women, and of wives in particular (Booth et al., 1984; Cherlin, 1981; Greene and Quester, 1982; Spitz and South, 1985). In addressing the association between wives' employment and marital dissolution, Cherlin (1981:53) wrote that, "almost every well-known scholar who had addressed this topic in the twentieth century has cited the importance of the increase in the employment of women" as a factor in the increase in divorce rates.

Two alternative, though not contradictory, explanations have been offered for the positive association between wives' employment and marital instability. One school of thought holds that there is something inherent in the employment of married women that may create strains and destabilize the traditional concept of a family. Another explanation is that wives' ability to support themselves outside of marriage may facilitate marital disruption by making divorce more attractive (Greenstein, 1990). However, as Goode (1956:72) wrote, "although popular opinion suggests that when the wife works the family is less likely to be stable, there is no conclusive evidence on this point" (see also Greenstein, 1990).

The present research is an attempt to assess the effects of indicators of wife's employment (employment status, occupational status, and relative earnings ratio) and religion (religious homogamy, religiosity, and religious versus civil marriage) on attitude toward divorce. Recent research has indicated that same-faith marriage, although declining, is still the norm (McCutcheon, 1988), and that religious assiduity and religious preference are associated with family dissolution (Heaton and Goodman, 1985). Research has further indicated that religious homogamy promotes marital stability. That is, if husband and wife have the same religious affiliation, divorce is less likely (Albrecht et al., 1983; Heaton et al., 1985). However, Heaton (1984) has noted that the effect of religious homogamy disappears, once frequency of religious attendance is taken into account. Consequently, alternative measures of religious factors are necessary to understand the connection between religion and family institutions.

DATA AND METHODS

Data

Data used in this paper were drawn from the Canadian Fertility Survey (CFS) conducted in April-June 1984. The CFS was Canada's first national fertility survey, using telephone interviews for both household selection and in-depth interviewing of the selected respondents, namely, women in the reproductive ages of 18 to 49 years. The total of 5,315 women of all marital statuses who were interviewed constitutes a nationally-representative sample. The overall response rate was 70 percent.

The survey questionnaire is an outgrowth not only of the World Fertility Survey (WFS) questionnaire, but of other surveys done in Canada, Europe and the United States. The CFS contained a substantial number of questions on attitudes toward marriage, family and abortion, seldom asked in fertility surveys. It also covered a wide range of topics, including pregnancy, marriage and work history, contraceptive behaviour, and socioeconomic background variables such as religion, education, income, and occupation, including those of the husband, where applicable.

For the present analysis, the sample was restricted to all married women who were still married to their first husband at the time of the survey, resulting in a sample of 3,049. Women in second or subsequent marriages were excluded since information on their attitude toward divorce is less meaningful; women whose marriages were disrupted may respond to the question differently than those whose marriages remained intact.

Variables

Dependent Variable

The dependent variable is attitude toward divorce. It is measured in response to the question, "In general, would you say you more or less agree or disagree with the statement: marriage is a permanent union which should only be broken for very serious reasons?" The responses are coded dichotomously, those reporting, "disagree" are coded as 0 and those reporting "agree" are coded as 1.

Independent Variables

The independent variables selected are typical of those frequently analyzed in studies on marital dissolution/instability (Becker, 1973; Booth, 1986; Greenstein, 1990; Heaton and Pratt, 1990; Mott and Moore, 1979; Shehan et al., 1990; White, 1990).

The sociodemographic variables included in the study are age (AGE), age at marriage (AGEMAR), number of children (CHILDREN), and years of schooling (EDUCATION). Past research suggests that older people, being more conservative, are more prone to marital stability. With regard to age at marriage, several studies have found a positive effect of young age at marriage on marital disruption (Moore and Waite, 1981; Becker et al., 1977; Booth and Edwards, 1985). Morgan and Rindfuss (1985) have emphasized the degree of change most individuals experience during the late teens and twenties which may create strains and make them more vulnerable to marital disruption. Presence of children has traditionally been found to be associated with more stable marriages, although there is some evidence of a negative link between the presence of children and marital stability. Some have argued that children hold families together either by increasing marital satisfaction or by making divorce more costly (Cherlin, 1977; Thornton, 1985). Others have suggested that children interfere with the husband-wife relationship (Campbell, 1975) and create strains that change the nature of the marital bond (Waite et al., 1985). With regard to education, past research suggests that the highly educated are less likely to opt for divorce (Mott and Moore, 1979; Moore and Waite, 1981; Bahr and Galligan, 1984).

Economic variables included in the study are employment status (EMPLOYMENT), occupational prestige (PRESTIGE), and relative earnings ratio (EARNING). Evidence implies that wives who are employed are more likely to report a positive attitude toward divorce (Booth et al., 1984; Spitz and South, 1985), since work outside the home creates both conflict and less spousal interaction. Net of employment status, occupational status appears to affect divorce attitudes; those with higher occupational status are more likely to report a positive attitude toward marital stability. For example, Greenstein (1990) suggested that wives who are employed as professionals, technical workers or managers are somewhat less likely to experience a marital disruption than are other workers. The empirical evidence regarding the effect of wives' earnings relative to total family earnings on marital dissolution is mixed. Moore and Waite (1981) found a positive effect of actual earnings ratio on marital dissolution. D'Amico (1983), however, found no effect of the ratio of actual incomes, although a positive effect was observed of relative potential income on marital stability among older women (aged 35-49).

The dimensions of religion included in the study are: religious homogamy (HOMOGAMY), religious assiduity (RELIGIOSITY), and religious/civil marriage (RELMAR). Homogamous couples, i.e., couples having the same religious affiliation and those who attend church services more often, are more likely to favour marriage as a permanent union (Heaton et al., 1985; Heaton and Pratt, 1990), since religious affiliation and participation may facilitate intimacy, communication, commitment, and the ability to overcome crisis (Abbott et al., 1990). Another dimension of religion that might affect divorce attitudes is religious/civil marriage. Although the exploration of this variable's influence on the family is theoretically important, there is no empirical evidence to support the hypothesis that religious marriage facilitates a positive attitude toward marital stability, and thus a healthy family, by enlarging the social support system available to the couple.

In this study, age, age at marriage, and number of children are measured as continuous variables. Years of schooling are used initially as a continuous variable and then as a dichotomous variable where 1 = 13 years of schooling or more. Employment status is measured by a dichotomous variable indicating whether wife works/seeking work outside the home (1) or not (0). Occupational prestige is the Blishen scores (Blishen and McRoberts, 1976) corresponding to occupation. Relative earnings ratio refers to wife's income as a proportion of family income. Religious homogamy is a dichotomous variable indicating whether couples belong to the same religion (1) or not (0). Religiosity is measured by the question, "How often do you attend religious services?" Responses ranged from "rarely/never" coded 0, to "weekly" coded 3. Religious marriage is measured by the question, "Did you marry in a religious ceremony?" Couples married in a religious ceremony are coded 1 and 0 otherwise.

As the dependent variable is dichotomous, a probit model to the dependent variable was fitted. Probit restricts predicted values to the range zero through one. Probit maximum likelihood estimates are more robust than those obtained through Ordinary Least Squares (OLS) but are identical to Ordinary Least Squares' unstandardized regression coefficients in interpretation.

RESULTS

Table 1 presents a brief description of the variables used in the analysis and the means and standard deviations. As the data in Table 1 indicate, the sample is heavily skewed toward religious homogamy and religious marriage. This means that these two variables cannot explain much of the variability in attitude toward divorce in the sample, even if the effects of these variables may be substantial.

Table 2 summarizes the results obtained in probit analysis of attitude toward divorce on labour force participation and selected sociodemographic characteristics.

Sociodemographic Variables

Contrary to expectations, age and age at marriage appear to have very little effect on divorce attitudes, holding other factors constant. Also, the presence of children does not affect divorce attitudes. Thus, there is no evidence that those who have children are more likely to favour marital permanence. The educational level of the woman appears to have a strong negative influence on attitude toward divorce indicating that highly educated women are less likely to view marriage as a permanent union, a finding that is the opposite of expectations. These findings suggest that the relationship between levels of schooling and attitude toward divorce is indeed nonlinear overall (Glenn and Supancic, 1984; Frisbie and Opitz, 1985). The variable was therefore dummy-coded, where 1 = 13 years of schooling or more and the analysis was repeated. The coefficients are again found strong and negative. Hence, well-educated wives appear to be less prone to marital permanence.

TABLE 1. Variables Included in the Analysis.

Variable	Abbreviation	Definition and Coding	Mean (SD)
Age	AGE	In years	34.11 (7.86)
Age at marriage	AGEMAR	In years	20.87 (3.46)
No. of children	CHILDREN	Number of children born alive to wife	2.01 (1.39)
Education	EDUCATION	In years of schooling completed by wife	12.37 (2.94)
Employment status	EMPLOYMENT	1 = Working or seeking work; 0 = Otherwise	66.89[a] (–)

Occupational prestige	PRESTIGE	In Blishen SEI scale units (Blishen and McRoberts, 1976)	45.60 (13.64)
Relative earnings ratio	EARNING	Wife's income as a proportion of family income	0.45 (0.30)
Religiosity	RELIGIOSITY	Frequency of church attendance 0 = Rarely/never; 1 = Few times a year, 2 = Monthly, 3 = Weekly	2.39 (1.39)
Religious homogamy	HOMOGAMY	1 = husband and wife have the same religious affiliation; 0 = Otherwise	79.47[a] (–)
Religious marriage	RELMARRIAGE	1 = Religious marriage; 0 = Civil	90.30[a] (–)

[a]Figures correspond to percentages for the category coded as 1.

TABLE 2. Unstandardized Regression Coefficients from Probit Analysis of Attitude Toward Divorce.

Variable	Before the interaction term is included	After the interaction term is included
AGE	−0.003	−0.002
	(0.006)	(0.006)
AGEMAR	0.006	0.006
	(0.011)	(0.011)
CHILDREN	0.040	0.037
	(0.034)	(0.034)
EDUCATION	−0.163**	−0.150**
	(0.075)	(0.075)
EMPLOYMENT	0.141**	0.242**
	(0.074)	(0.100)

EMPINCOME	–	–0.145*
		(0.096)
PRESTIGE	0.001	0.002
	(0.003)	(0.003)
RELIGIOSITY	0.106**	0.104**
	(0.026)	(0.026)
HOMOGAMY	–0.222**	–0.220**
	(0.090)	(0.090)
RELMAR	0.050	0.051
	(0.118)	(0.118)
Intercept	3.844	3.893

Notes: 1. Standard errors are presented in parentheses.
2. The variable EARNING was dropped from the analysis because it did not reach statistical significance.
3. EDUCATION is recoded into a categorical variable as 1 = 13+ years of schooling.

*$p < .05$ **$p < .01$

Economic Variables

As we see in Table 2, wife's employment status is positively strongly related to attitude toward divorce. This effect is intriguing, since findings from previous studies indicate that wife's employment has a positive effect on marital instability. The positive effect may suggest that the increased economic security due to the wife's employment may outweigh any negative effects, perhaps by reducing the stress associated with economic hardship, resulting in more favourable responses to view marriage as a permanent union. This suggests an interaction between income and employment status. To distinguish between higher and lower income families, a dummy variable EMPINCOME (defined as 1 for wives whose family income was above $30,000) was employed. It is assumed that high family income couples with wives working outside the home would be significantly more likely to see marriages as permanent unions. The effect of the interaction term, however, does not provide support for our hypothesis; the results reveal that high income couples with wives working outside the home would be less likely to consider marriage as a permanent union. Higher occupational status is also associated with a more positive attitude toward marital permanence, although the variable does not reach statistical significance.

Religious Variables

Religiosity has significant effects on attitude toward divorce. Wives who attend church services more frequently are more likely to report a positive attitude toward marital permanence than those who attend church services less frequently. Religious marriage does not have statistically significant impacts on the dependent variable when other factors are taken into account, but it does provide some support for our hypothesis. Additional research may be warranted to support the hypothesis that those who married in a religious ceremony are more likely to report a positive attitude toward marital permanence.

Contrary to expectations, the data show that wives in same-faith marriages report more disagreement over "marriage is a permanent union which should only be broken for very serious reasons." The results indicate that those who are with common religious orientations have about the same odds of being in unstable marriages.

CONCLUSIONS

In this research, the Canadian Fertility Survey data were used to investigate the effects of selected sociodemographic, economic and religious variables on attitude toward divorce. Of the factors considered in this research, wife's employment status, education, religiosity, and religious homogamy have the largest effect on divorce attitudes. Regarding the central focus of our inquiry, the overall effect of wives' employment on attitude toward divorce appears to be substantial, and the evidence indicates a positive link between wives' employment and their attitude toward marital permanence. By incorporating several relevant control variables into the analysis, we have been able to provide a more refined estimate of the net impact of wife's employment on attitude toward divorce.

The less educated and those who are employed are more likely to agree that marriage is a permanent union which should only be broken for very serious reasons. These findings are consistent with some of the earlier research on marital instability (e.g., Booth et al., 1984). At the same time, attitude toward divorce is strongly related to religious factors, especially religiosity. Clearly, then, reliance on sociodemographic and economic factors in explaining attitude toward divorce would be inadequate.

One limitation must be kept in mind when analyzing these results. The data on attitude toward divorce permitted only a simple dichotomy, thereby precluding a thorough analysis because dichotomization ignores variations in the dependent variables (Heaton and Pratt, 1990). In addition, the CFS data contain no information to measure marital quality and satisfaction. The analysis was, of course, limited by the data in the degree to which we could explain attitude toward marital permanence in terms of its correlates. Still, the pattern of associations of variables, such as employment and religion, is interesting. The patterns of associations for these variables suggest that marriages are viewed differently by employed and religious wives than by their counterparts and that ending of the marriage may have different socioeconomic determinants, socially, in particular.

The results indicate, strictly speaking, that positive attitude toward marital permanence is stronger among the less educated, employed, highly religious, and those couples who have different religious orientations. The role of children on attitude toward divorce may be much less than once thought. It is also premature to conclude that an increase in interreligious marriages has contributed to an increase in divorce in recent years. It appears that homogamy within marriage apparently does not keep couples from considering divorce. However, as Glenn (1982:565) has suggested, "it appears that the increases in heterogamy and in divorce probably both reflect some of the same underlying changes in the institution of marriage." This leaves important questions for family sociologists: What social conditions contribute to marital dissolution?

REFERENCES

Abbott, D. A., M. Berry, and W. H. Meredith (1990). Religious belief and practice: A potential asset in helping families. *Family Relations*, 39, 443-48.

Albrecht, S. L., H. M. Bahr, and K. L. Goodman (1983). *Divorce and Remarriage*. Westport, CT: Greenwood.

Bahr, S. J. and R. J. Galligan (1984). Teenage marriage and marital stability. *Youth and Society*, 15, 387-400.

Becker, G. S. (1973). A theory of marriage: Part I. *Journal of Political Economy*, July/August, 813-47.

Becker, G. S., E. M. Landes, and R. T. Michael (1977). An economic analysis of marital instability. *Journal of Political Economy*, 85, 1141-87.

Blishen, B. R. and H. A. McRoberts (1976). A revised socioeconomic index for occupations in Canada. *Canadian Review of Sociology and Anthropology*, 13, February, 71-79.

Booth, A. D., R. Johnson, L. White, and J. N. Edwards (1984). Women, outside employment, and marital instability. *American Journal of Sociology*, 90, 567-83.

Booth, A. and J. N. Edwards (1985). Age at marriage and marital instability. *Journal of Marriage and the Family*, 47, 67-75.

Campbell, A. (1975). The American way of mating: Marriage si, children only maybe. *Psychology Today*, May, 37-43.

Cherlin, A. J. (1977). The effect of children on marital dissolution. *Demography*, 44, 265-72.

Cherlin A. J. (1981). *Marriage, Divorce, and Remarriage*. Cambridge, MA: Harvard University Press.

D'Amico, R. (1983). Status maintenance or status competition? Wife's relative wage as a determinant of labour supply and marital instability. *Social Forces*, 61, 1186-1205.

Frisbie, W. P. and W. Optiz (1985). Race/ethnic and gender differentials in marital instability: 1980. Paper presented at the Population Association of America Meetings, March.

Glenn, N. D. and M. Supancic (1984). Sociological and demographic correlates of divorce and separation in the United States: An update and reconsideration. *Journal of Marriage and the Family*, 46, 563-76.

Goode, W. J. (1956). *After Divorce*. New York: Free Press.

Greene, W. H. and A. O. Quester (1982). Divorce risk and wives' labour supply behaviour. *Social Science Quarterly*, 63, 16-27.

Greenstein, T. N. (1990). Marital disruption and the employment of married women. *Journal of Marriage and the Family*, 52 (August), 657-76.

Heaton, T. B. (1984). Religious homogamy and marital satisfaction reconsidered. *Journal of Marriage and the Family*, 46, 729-33.

Heaton, T. B., S. L. Albrecht, and T. K. Martin (1985). The timing of divorce. *Journal of Marriage and the Family*, 47, 631-39.

Heaton, T. B. and K. L. Goodman (1985). Religion and family formation. *Review of Religious Research*, 26, 343-59.

Heaton, T. B. and E. L. Pratt (1990). The effects of religious homogamy on marital satisfaction and stability. *Journal of Family Issues*, 11, 2, 191-207.

McCutcheon, A. L. (1988). Denominations and religious intermarriage: Trends among white Americans in the twentieth century. *Review of Religious Research*, 29, 216-27.

Moore, K. A. and L. J. Waite (1981). Marital dissolution, early motherhood, and early marriage. *Social Forces*, 60, 20-40.

Morgan, S. P. and R. R. Rindfuss (1985). Marital disruption: Structural and temporal dimensions. *American Journal of Sociology*, 90, 1055-77.

Mott, F. L. and S. F. Moore (1979). The causes of marital disruption among young American women: An interdisciplinary perspective. *Journal of Marriage and the Family*, May, 355-365.

Shehan, C. L., E. W. Bock, and G. R. Lee (1990). Religious heterogamy, religiosity, and marital happiness: The case of Catholics. *Journal of Marriage and the Family*, 52, 73-79.

Spitz, G. and S. J. South (1985). Women's employment, time expenditure, and divorce. *Journal of Family Issues*, 6, 307-29.

Thornton, A. (1985). Changing attitudes toward separation and divorce: Causes and consequences. *American Journal of Sociology*, 90, 856-72.

Thwing, C. F. and C. F. B. Thwing (1986). *The Family: A Historical and Social Study*. Boston: Lee and Shepard.

Townson, M. (1987). Women's labour force participation, fertility rates, and the implications for economic development and government policy. Discussion paper, 87.A.11. Ottawa, Ontario: Studies in Social Policy.

Waite, L. J., G. W. Haggstrom, and D. E. Kanouse (1985). The consequences of parenthood for the marital stability of young adults. *American Sociological Review*, 50, 850-57.

Remarried Families' Economic Behavior: Fishman's Model Revisited

Jean M. Lown
Elizabeth M. Dolan

INTRODUCTION

> Economic behavior expresses–both actually and symbolically–a remarried couple's commitment to one another and to each other's children. (Fishman, 1983: 359)

Every married couple must decide how to manage their finances. One of the first decisions is whether to combine all income and assets into joint accounts or to maintain separate accounts. Research and clinical studies suggest that decisions regarding resource allocation and control can be more complex for remarried couples than for couples in a first marriage (Duberman, 1975; Fishman, 1983; Messinger, 1976; Visher & Visher, 1979). Integrating the financial affairs of two families is often problematic for remarried couples; in fact, children and finances are two of the most stressful

Jean M. Lown, PhD, is Professor, Department of Human Environments, Utah State University, Logan, UT 84322-2910. Elizabeth M. Dolan, PhD, is Associate Professor, Department of Family Studies, Pettee Hall, University of New Hampshire, Durham, NH 03824-3599.

Partial research support was provided by the College of Family Life and Office of Vice President for Research, Utah State University and the University of New Hampshire Agricultural Research Station.

[Haworth co-indexing entry note]: "Remarried Families' Economic Behavior: Fishman's Model Revisited." Lown, Jean M., and Elizabeth M. Dolan. Co-published simultaneously in *Journal of Divorce & Remarriage* (The Haworth Press, Inc.) Vol. 22, No. 1/2, 1994, pp. 103-119; and: *The Economics of Divorce: The Effects on Parents and Children* (ed: Craig A. Everett) The Haworth Press, Inc., 1994, pp. 103-119. Multiple copies of this article/chapter may be purchased from The Haworth Document Delivery Center [1-800-3-HAWORTH; 9:00 a.m. - 5:00 p.m. (EST)].

aspects of remarried family life (Fishman, 1983; Ganong & Coleman, 1989; Messinger, 1976). Despite recognition of this problem, research on any aspect of financial management in remarriage is scant.

This study re-examines Fishman's (1983) common-pot versus two-pot framework for economic behavior of remarried couples. Instead of employing the exchange theory, as Fishman did, this study examines economic behavior in terms of family adaptability and cohesion.

Financial Resources

In America most married couples pool their financial resources (Blumstein & Schwartz, 1983), that is, they combine all income from whatever source into a single pool of funds from which all household and family members' financial needs are serviced. However, the pervasiveness of this financial structure, or its alternatives, has not been well documented. Blumstein and Schwartz (1983) have furnished some insight by comparing the economic behavior of married, unmarried, heterosexual and homosexual couples. They estimated that 8-18% of all types of couples maintain completely separate accounts, that is, combine none of their financial resources into a single account. These researchers concluded that the handling of financial resources is symbolic of the commitment to the relationship as well as the individuals' desire for equality and autonomy. Married couples especially appeared to view financial interdependence, or the commingling of their money, as a symbol of mutual trust. Unmarried couples were striving for more independence within their relationships and avoidance of conflict that the intermingling of financial resources might bring, and thus were much more likely to keep their financial resources separate (Blumstein & Schwartz, 1983).

The question of whether or not to intermingle economic resources in marriage is a relatively new one. Research reports from twenty or thirty years ago on couples' economic behavior do not even acknowledge the possibility of maintaining completely separate financial resources (e.g., Kyrk, 1953; Wells, 1959; Ferber & Lee, 1974). Now that many partners both have their own income through employment, and in the case of remarried couples financial ties to other households, the question of financial interdependence becomes relevant. This consideration may be more likely to arise in a remarriage than a first marriage because financial resources frequently have to meet the demands of additional family members in multiple households. Undependable child support and unanticipated requests for money by nonresidential children can complicate financial arrangements and planning. Resentment of child support and/or spousal support obligations are potential areas of conflict between remarried spouses (Dahl, Cowgill & Asmundsson, 1987).

Fishman (1983) proposed a dichotomous model of complete intermingling or joint accounts versus separate accounts based on exchange theory and commitment to marriage to explain the economic behavior of remarried couples. She postulated that the joint or "common-pot" style contributed to stepfamily integration and was typical where finances were tight and former spouses were not paying child support. Separate accounts or "two-pot" couples tended to be more affluent with nonresidential fathers paying child support and participating to a greater degree in the lives of their children from their previous marriage. In the two-pot families each spouse contributed to specified household needs, reserving their remaining incomes for themselves and their biological children. Fishman concluded that the joint or common-pot approach fostered family unity while the separate accounts method encouraged individual autonomy. Coleman and Ganong (1989) found no connection between pooling and marital closeness, although adults who pooled their finances felt slightly closer to the children in their household.

Although eight of the 16 remarried couples in the Fishman study kept separate accounts, it is unlikely that half of all remarried couples actually adopt this model. None of the 22 remarried couples in a study by Lown (1984) had adopted a separate accounts system. In a study of 105 remarried couples, Coleman and Ganong (1989) reported that 74% indicated they pool incomes and share expenses.

Fishman presented her model as a dichotomy of completely joint or pooled accounts versus separate accounts. Coleman and Ganong (1989) also used the dichotomous model and relied on only one question to determine group membership (pool versus two pot). Other research (Dolan, 1989) suggests that financial arrangements are more accurately and realistically conceptualized as a continuum with totally pooled funds and completely separate accounts representing the two extremes with many variations in between. Couples often combine elements of the two systems such as maintaining separate checking and/or savings accounts in addition to joint checking and/or savings.

Whereas commingling of financial assets has been the norm for nuclear families, remarried families may need a more flexible approach. Due to their family situation, remarried couples may be more likely to follow a less traditional model of financial organization than couples in a first marriage. Coleman and Ganong (1989) found that households where only one spouse was a stepparent were more likely to combine their financial assets into one pot than those households where both spouses were stepparents. While commingling or pooling of financial resources appears to be a popular choice among remarried couples according to the findings of Lown (1984), Coleman and Ganong (1989), and even Fishman (1983), how prevalent is this method among remarried couples? Are more cohesive remarried couples more likely than less cohesive remarried couples to pool their financial affairs?

Conceptual Framework

Examining remarried family financial organization in the context of family cohesion and adaptability provides another dimension of understanding family interaction (Olson, 1986; Pill, 1990). The concept of family cohesion is defined as "the emotional bonding that family members have toward one another," and family adaptability is defined as "the ability of a marital or family system to change its power structure, role relationship, and relationship rules in response to situational and developmental stress" (Olson, Russell & Sprenkle, 1983, p. 48). Both of these concepts may be related to a couple's decisions regarding their financial organization.

Family scholars have developed models for family interaction based on the nuclear family. How well these models fit the remarried family is currently being explored (e.g., Pill, 1990). Studies using the cohesion/adaptability framework of the Circumplex Model have yielded conflicting results. Olson's Circumplex Model (Olson, 1986) is based on the assumption that functional families will be balanced in their bonding and role relationships. Families with extreme scores in one or both dimensions are likely to be dysfunctional. Pill (1990) concluded that comparing stepfamilies with nuclear families results in negative connotations regarding stepfamily functioning. The studies which have examined stepfamily cohesion have consistently found them to be much less cohesive than nuclear families (Bray, Berger, Silverblatt & Hollier, 1987; Peek, Bell, Waldren & Sorell, 1988; Pill, 1990). Bray et al. (1987) found that stepfamilies did not differ from nuclear families in adaptability. On the other hand, Peek et al. (1988) found stepfamilies to be less adaptable, and Pill (1990) found them to be more adaptable. Furthermore, Pill (1990) found that the stepfamilies scoring in the less cohesive, more adaptable range also scored higher in marital satisfaction. Pill concluded that although high adaptability and low cohesion may be undesirable in a nuclear family, these same traits may promote healthy stepfamily functioning.

Objectives

The purpose of this study was to examine Fishman's framework of economic behavior of remarried couples in the context of family cohesion and adaptability. Additionally, the study was designed to ascertain whether a common-pot versus two-pot dichotomy of economic behavior exists or if another alternative, a combination of maintaining both joint and separate accounts, is also used, and the prevalence of these strategies. Can remarried families' economic behavior be differentiated on the basis of receipt of child support, family income, perceived income adequacy and wife's employment as described by Fishman? Will couples who pool their financial resources score lower on adaptability than other couples? Will they be more cohesive than other remarried couples?

If Fishman's conceptualization is valid, then couples who pool their financial resources should be more cohesive than those adopting alternate strategies. This would also be consistent with the conclusions of Blumstein and Schwartz (1983). While Fishman did not specifically address couple adaptability, Pill (1990) concluded that healthy, well functioning stepfamilies may be more adaptable than first marriages. Thus, one might expect that those couples adopting a separate accounts strategy should score higher on adaptability because they may have more complex family backgrounds and present needs requiring a creative approach to financial management.

METHOD

Sample

Data were collected in 1986 from remarried couples residing in four states with diverse populations: Kentucky, New Hampshire, Utah and Wyoming. A couple was eligible to participate if at least one of the spouses had been previously married. Names of remarried couples were obtained from state vital statistics records except in New Hampshire where these records are not public information. The New Hampshire sample was identified through stepparenting workshops followed by the snowball technique: participating couples were asked to provide names of other remarried couples.

Data Collection

A mailed survey followed by a telephone interview developed according to the Dillman (1978) Total Design Method were used to collect the data. A pilot study (Lown, 1984) determined that dual data collection instruments were the most effective way to obtain responses to the large number and variety of questions. Cohesion and adaptability were measured using the Family Adaptability and Cohesion Evaluation Scale, or FACES III (Olson, 1986). FACES III is a 20-item paper-and-pencil instrument designed to measure respondent perception of family cohesion and adaptability. Demographic information, FACES III and objective questions on financial management were included in the mailed instrument; the telephone interview dealt with the more subjective and sensitive questions on financial matters.

Current addresses were located using marriage license data, telephone directories and city directories. Subjects were initially contacted by telephone and invited to participate in the study. Current addresses were confirmed and the survey instruments were mailed to each spouse. A letter explaining the study was mailed, along with the instruments, to couples who could not be contacted by phone. When the mailed surveys were returned, the subjects were contacted to arrange separate, private phone interviews which lasted about 45 minutes to one hour.

Data Analysis

Interview data indicated that Fishman's dichotomous model of economic behavior is too simplistic. Based on responses from the sample, the dichotomous model was replaced by a modified model consisting of three economic strategies: pooled or joint accounts; completely separate accounts; and a combination, or mixed, strategy of joint and separate accounts. Couples were assigned to one of the three categories of financial organization based on their responses to a series of questions about how they handled their income, savings and expenditures. If both spouses indicated that they pooled all or almost all their financial resources, they were assigned to the "pooled" (common-pot) category; if both indicated that they kept all or almost all their finances separate, they were assigned to the "separate accounts" (two-pot) category; if either of the spouses indicated that they kept some finances separate while pooling others, the couple was assigned to the "mixed" category. Thus, couples were divided into three categories of financial management rather than dichotomous categories.

Several demographic variables used by Fishman to classify her stepfamilies were also included in these analyses; these included family income, employment of wife, and receipt of child support. Perceived income adequacy was included as well, since Fishman (1983) reported that low-to-moderate income couples were most likely to adopt a common pot system while higher income couples used separate accounts.

To obtain an indication of family adaptability and cohesion using FACES III, responses by each spouse to the ten items relating to adaptability and cohesion were summed. The mean score for the couple is derived by averaging the husband's and wife's scores (Olson, Portner & Lavee, 1985). Where a response to a single item was missing, the respondent's mean score was substituted for the missing response. Respondents who failed to answer more than one item were eliminated from these analyses. Complete FACES data were available for 84% of the pooling couples, 75% of the mixed style couples and 100% of the separate accounts couples.

The chi-square test of independence was used to measure the strength of the association between the three family demographic variables identified as important by Fishman and the three categories of financial organization.

RESULTS

Description of the Sample

Useable data were collected from 116 remarried couples who had been in their current marriage for no more than ten years. The length of the current marriage ranged from less than one year to ten years with a mean of 2.4 years (s.d. = 20.1 months). The mean age of the wives was 35.8 years (s.d. = 7.4) and 37.5 years (s.d. = 8.15) for husbands. For 71% of the couples, the current marriage was a remarriage for both partners, the majority of whom had been divorced. Only ten couples did not have children. For the 106 couples with children, the mean was 3.4 per family (s.d. = 2.0) and the range was one to ten.

In three quarters (77%) of these families both spouses were employed. None of the separate accounts couples were single-earner couples; 21.9% of the mixed and 27.4% of poolers were single-earner families. Only 13% of wives were full-time homemakers, most of whom were poolers. An additional 6% of wives and 8% of husbands were retired, unemployed or students. Median family income was in the $30,000-$39,999 range (median family income in the U.S. was approximately $30,000 the year these data were collected) (U.S. Bureau of Census, 1989). Most of the families with children were either stepfather families (35.3%), had no children currently living in their household (30.5%), or had only their own (mutual) children living at home (15.5%).

Styles of Financial Organization

Seventy-four of the 116 couples (63.8%) pooled their financial resources (Fishman's common-pot framework). Ten couples (8.6%)

maintained separate accounts (two-pot framework). The remaining 32 couples (27.6%) used a combination of joint and separate accounts (mixed). While remarried couples employ a variety of financial strategies, fully two-thirds of this sample subscribe to the traditional model of pooling their financial affairs; while slightly more than a quarter combined joint and separate accounts.

Common-pot style: poolers. The 74 couples who adopted this financial strategy had a median family income of $30,000-$39,000, had been in their current marriage an average of 2.5 years (s.d. = 21.6 months), and had a mean of 3.4 children (s.d. = 2.0). Six out of the ten childless couples were in this group in addition to almost two-thirds of those where one spouse was married for the first time. About half of those who had been widowed were poolers. Eighty-one percent of all the homemaker couples were in this group. Likewise, most of those couples where one spouse was employed part-time were financial poolers: 58% of all the part-time employed wives and 83% of all the part-time employed husbands. Forty-seven percent of these families were receiving child support.

Two-pot style: separate accounts. The ten couples who kept their finances separate had been married for the shortest time (M = 1.9 years; s.d. = 20.5 months). In 9 of the 10 couples, both spouses had been previously divorced; one person was married for the first time. All of these couples were dual-earners with a mean income of $30,000-$39,999. Contrary to Fishman's framework, these couples were not the highest income group. This group had the highest level of educational attainment (median = college graduate for both husbands and wives). While all ten families had children, they had the lowest mean number of children per family (M = 2.8; s.d = 1.5). Four of 10 families were receiving child support.

Combination style: mixed. The couples who adopted a mixed strategy for organizing their financial assets had been married an average of 2.25 years (s.d. = 16.4 months). Four families were childless; those who had children averaged 3.35 children per family. Only 39% of those families with children were receiving child support. This group had the highest median income of the three groups ($40,000-$49,999). Twenty-two percent were single-earner couples. The remaining half of the spouses who had been previously widowed were in this group.

Comparison with Fishman's Results

The picture presented by these results does not coincide with that presented by Fishman (1983). With over 60% of the sample pooling all of their economic resources and less than 10% maintaining completely separate accounts, the financial organization of remarried couples appears to be more traditional than Fishman described.

Fishman reported that the separate accounts families had much higher incomes than the poolers; in this study the groups had similar incomes. Chi square analysis revealed no significant difference among the three groups ($\chi^2 = 5.57$) when income level was divided into two categories (above or below the U.S. median of $30,000).

A major distinction between the common-pot and two-pot families in the Fishman study was the adequacy of their financial resources. The common-pot families had substantial discretionary income. Since perceived income adequacy may be a better predictor of financial satisfaction than objective measures (Winter, Bivens & Morris, 1984), chi square was used to compare husbands' and wives' perceived income adequacy in relation to their chosen method of financial organization. Again, the outcome revealed no significant differences among the groups (husband $\chi^2 = 4.08$, $p < .396$; wife $\chi^2 = 6.78$, $p < .567$).

All eight of the common-pot families in the Fishman study were dual-earner households; the several homemaker households were two-pot families. Based on this finding, we would expect to find a relationship between financial organization style and the employment of the wife. A chi square value of 4.42 ($p < .353$) indicated no differences among the groups on this variable. The majority of those who were one-earner families in this sample were, in fact, poolers, and all the couples keeping separate accounts were dual earners.

Fishman reported that common-pot families were more likely than two-pot families to receive child support. A chi square test of independence revealed no significant differences among the three groups regarding the receipt of child support ($\chi^2 = .314$, $p < .85$). Less than half of all families (45.2%) in the study received child support, varying from 39% of couples using the mixed strategy to 47% of the pooling couples.

In conclusion, couples did not differ demographically based on their choice of financial organization. Contrary to Fishman's findings, there appears to be no relationship between receipt of child support, family income, perceived income adequacy, or wife's employment status and economic behavior in remarried couples.

Cohesion and Adaptability

Relying on exchange theory, Fishman emphasized that economic behavior was indicative of a couple's commitment to marriage. The common-pot couples were characterized as being more committed to family unity, while the two-pot couples valued individual autonomy. In an effort to test Fishman's hypothesis regarding the link between financial management style and commitment to family unity, we substituted the concept of cohesion as measured by FACES III. Common-pot couples were expected to score highest on cohesion with two-pot couples scoring lowest of the three groups. Couple cohesion as defined by FACES III is measured by their mean score and plotted onto one of four levels over a continuum: disengaged, separated, connected or enmeshed.

Since separate pot financial management varies the most from the norm or ideal of the common pot for married couple we expected the ten separate pot couples to score highest on adaptability. Couple adaptability is evaluated similarly on four levels over a continuum: rigid, structured, flexible or chaotic. The scores of balanced couples fall in the middle categories (separated/connected and structured/flexible), while dysfunctional couples tend to be on the extremes (disengaged/enmeshed and rigid/chaotic). Therefore, extrapolating from Fishman's premise, one might expect that couples who choose a more nontraditional method of financial organization, i.e., separate accounts, would be less cohesive and more adaptable in their family functioning. Similarly, those who pool their financial assets would be expected to score in the less flexible, more cohesive ranges of family functioning.

Those couples who chose the separate accounts method of financial organization do indeed appear to be more adaptable. Ninety percent of these couples scored in the flexible or chaotic range. The mean score for this group (27.45) is very close to the chaotic range. The group exhibiting the least adaptability, perhaps somewhat surprisingly, was the mixed financial organization group with only 36.4% in the flexible/chaotic range and a mean score (24.42) in the structured range.

The mean cohesion score of pooling couples (X = 40.11) indicates that they are slightly more cohesive than either the mixed financial organization couples (X = 38.32) or the separate accounts couples (X = 38.9), both of which fall into the separated range. While not a substantial difference, those couples who pool their financial assets scored more frequently in the connected/enmeshed range (52.8%) than did those who adopted separate accounts (40%) or adopted a mixed strategy (32.3%). Couples in the mixed financial organization group had the greatest number in the disengaged range (19.4%) than either the pooling or separate accounts couples (18.1% and 10% respectively). Of those who pooled, 12.5% scored in the enmeshed range, while only 3.2% of those who adopted a mixed strategy and none of those who adopted separate accounts scored in that range. Comparing the mean scores of these couples to Pill's (1990) results and the norms for FACES III (Olson et al., 1985), scores of these couples are more similar to the norm (nuclear families) than to Pill's adolescent stepfamilies. Pill found her stepfamilies with adolescents to be much more adaptable (X = 27.2) and much less cohesive (X = 33.9) than the norm for nuclear families with adolescents. The mean score for adaptability for this sample of remarried couples was 24.9 (ranging from 24.4 to 27.4 by economic behavior) which is very similar to the Olson's norm for couples in nuclear families (X = 24.1). The couples who maintain separate accounts alone are more similar to Pill's couples. The mean cohesion score for the total sample is 39.3, and the norm for couples in nuclear families is 39.8 (Olson et al., 1985).

DISCUSSION AND CONCLUSIONS

The primary objective of this study was to test Fishman's exchange framework of financial management in remarriage. Did Fishman's conceptualization of remarried couples' economic behavior reflect actual practice for a larger, more diverse sample? Although Fishman conceptualized financial management in terms of a dichotomy of pooling or separate accounts, financial organization is more accurately and realistically conceptualized as a continuum with total pooling and completely separate accounts representing the two extremes. Despite the desirability of using a continuum to describe financial organization, an instrument to measure such a continuum remains to be developed. Results of the interviews suggested that three categories of financial management are more appropriate than two.

The results of this study indicate that while pooling of financial resources is the choice for the majority of remarried couples, the nuclear, common-pot family model is not the definitive method of financial organization. Remarried couples appear to be willing to craft a financial system which will meet their unique needs and philosophies about the meaning of marriage the second time around. Further, pooling of all finances does not suit all remarried couples. Each of the alternatives has strengths which may facilitate remarried couple functioning. As Blumstein and Schwartz (1983) noted, when it comes to pooling finances, some couples cannot imagine it while others cannot envision life any other way.

The results of this investigation did not reveal the same demographic differences in remarried couples' financial organization that Fishman reported. Median level of income was not higher for those who kept the accounts separate than for those who pooled. Couples who kept separate accounts were not more likely to be receiving child support than those who pooled. Neither were there any differences based on perceived adequacy of income or employment of wife. The results of this study suggest that the choice of financial organization is not related to remarried couple demographics.

Financial organization decisions in remarriage may be related to a couple's family needs and their ability to be flexible. Couples who keep their financial accounts separate do so for a reason and tend to be rather adaptable in their family interaction. Couple cohesion also appears to be related to choice of financial organization. As might be expected, those couples who kept their accounts separate were much less cohesive than the other two groups. The need to be financially bound to their partner was less for those who chose to pool or to use a combination approach to financial organization. Overall, those couples who are more cohesive and less adaptable appear to be more likely to pool their financial assets. However, when the means scores for both cohesion and adaptability are compared with the norms for couples in nuclear families, the difference is negligible.

The findings support Fishman's assertions that poolers are more cohesive. Those couples who pooled all of their financial assets were more likely to score in the high cohesion ranges of the continuum than the other couples, indicating they are slightly more emotionally bonded. For remarried couples, being less cohesive may be less a sign of loose commitment to the family and more a response to the need to address the complex financial (and other) needs of a remarried family.

The results of this study call into question the opening quotation from Fishman. To a certain extent economic behavior may reflect commitment to the remarried family. But in a larger context economic behavior reflects the potential complex financial needs and obligations of the new family. Consequently, our major recommendation is that educators and counselors should encourage couples to discuss finances and explore alternatives to the common pot system prior to and during remarriage. Remarried couples may indeed be more adaptable than nuclear families (Pill, 1990) and thus open to exploring alternative methods of financial organization. "(I)t is not very romantic or interesting to talk about net worth or projections of income or one's indebtedness, so money becomes the last frontier of self-disclosure even though each partner may hold strong feelings about how money should be dealt with" (Blumstein & Schwartz, 1983, p. 51). Due to the complex financial obligations which can arise in a remarriage, establishing a system which meets the remarried couple's individual needs and preferences regarding financial control as well as the actual financial demands of the remarried family may necessitate a nontraditional strategy.

Tempering these recommendations is the knowledge that few remarried adults use the services of family professionals to prepare for remarriage (Ganong & Coleman, 1989). This conclusion is consistent with a study that found that persons who experienced financial problems which contributed to their divorce were highly unlikely to discuss finances prior to remarriage (Lown, 1984).

Ganong and Coleman (1989) recommended improving the marketing of educational and counseling services for remarried families. Because few family life educators have expertise in financial management, additional training in this area and cooperative efforts with family financial educators and advisors may enhance the quality of services for remarried couples. Specific recommendations for financial management workshops are available elsewhere (Lown, McFadden & Crossman, 1989). Cooperative Extension Service adult educators may be eager to expand their programming to meet the needs of remarried families and therefore may be willing to collaborate with family life educators and counselors to develop workshops. Building coalitions of professionals serving the needs of families is the most promising way to reach out to remarried families.

The model for both financial organization and for family functioning has often been the nuclear family. The needs and stresses in a remarried family, however, may necessitate the adoption of a nontraditional, alternative method of financial organization. As Pill (1990) indicated, the ability to adapt to changing financial and household conditions may be a key characteristic of successful stepfamilies. The remarried couples in this study appear to be adaptable in tailoring their economic behavior to meet their needs.

One limitation of the study is the cross sectional nature of the data. Future research should follow newly remarried couples over a period of years to determine whether they adjust their financial management practices over the years of their marriage. Perhaps couples who initially maintain two separate pots may move toward pooling over time as their relationship solidifies. One might expect that respondents represent only those remarriages which are happy and successful; unhappy couples might have been over-represented among the refusals and those couples we were unable to locate.

Future research should employ a more sophisticated instrument for measuring financial management style. Use of such a tool in a longitudinal study would enable researchers to explore the question of whether financial management style is linked to success of the remarriage.

REFERENCES

Blumstein, P. & Schwartz, P. (1983). *American couples: Money, work, sex*. New York: William Morrow & Co.

Bray, J. H., Berger, S. H., Silverblatt, A. H., & Hollier, A. (1987). Family process and organization during remarriage: A preliminary analysis. In J. P. Vincent (Ed.), *Advances in Family Intervention, Assessment and Theory, Vol. 4* (pp. 253-279). Greenwich, CT: JAI Press.

Coleman, M. & Ganong, L. H. (1989). Financial management in stepfamilies. *Lifestyles: Family and Economic Issues, 10*, 217-232.

Dahl, A. S., Cowgill, K. M., & Asmundsson, R. (1987). Life in remarriage families. *Social Work, 32*, 40-44.

Dillman, D. A. (1978). *Mail and telephone surveys: the total design method*. New York: John Wiley & Sons.

Dolan, E. M. (1989). Financial management in remarriage. In R. Walker (Ed.), *Families in Transition: Structural Changes and Effects on Family Life. Proceedings of the 1989 Family Economics-Home Management Section Pre-Conference Workshop of the American Home Economics Association* (pp. 76-80). Cincinnati, OH: American Home Economics Association.

Duberman, L. (1975). *The reconstituted family: A study of remarried couples and their children*. Chicago, IL: Nelson-Hall Publishers.

Ferber, R. & Lee, L. C. (1974). Husband-Wife Influence in Family Purchasing Behavior. *Journal of Consumer Research, 1*, 43-50.

Fishman, B. (1983). The economic behavior of stepfamilies. *Family Relations, 32*, 359-366.

Ganong, L. H. & Coleman, M. (1989). Preparing for remarriage: Anticipating the issues, seeking solutions. *Family Relations, 38*, 28-33.

Kyrk, H. (1953). *The Family in the American Economy*. Chicago: University of Chicago Press.

Lown, J. M. (1984). Financial management practices of remarried families. In C. A. Dickson (Ed.), *Proceedings of the Western Regional Home Management-Family Economics Educators* (pp. 52-56). Honolulu, HI: Western Regional Home Management-Family Economics Educators.

Lown, J. M., McFadden, J. R., & Crossman, S. (1989). Family life education for remarriage: Focus on financial management. *Family Relations, 38*, 40-45.

Messinger, L. (1976). Remarriage between divorced people with children from previous marriages: A proposal for preparation for remarriage. *Journal of Marriage and Family Counseling, 2*, 193-200.

Olson, D. H. (1986). Circumplex model VII: Validation studies and FACES III. *Family Process, 25*, 337-351.

Olson, D. H., Russell, C. S., & Sprenkle, D. H. (1983). Circumplex model VI: Theoretical update. *Family Process, 22*, 69-83.

Olson, D. H., Portner, J., & Lavee, Y. (1985). *FACES III*. St. Paul, MN: Family Social Science, University of Minnesota.

Peek, C. W., Bell, N. J., Waldren, T., & Sorell, G. T. (1988). Patterns of functioning in families of remarried and first-married couples. *Journal of Marriage and the Family, 50,* 699-708.

Pill, C. J. (1990). Stepfamilies: Redefining the Family. *Family Relations, 39,* 186-193.

U.S. Bureau of the Census (1989). *Studies in Marriage and the Family* (Current Population Reports, Series P-23, No. 162). Washington, DC: U. S. Government Printing Office.

Visher, E. & Visher, J. (1979). *Stepfamilies: A guide to working with stepparents and stepchildren.* New York: Brunner/Mazel.

Wells, H. L. (1959). Financial Management Practices of Young Families. *Journal of Home Economics, 51,* 439-443.

Winter, M., Bivens, G., & Morris, E. (1984). The assessment of subjective change in family financial well-being. In G. Rowe (Ed.), *Family Strengths 5: Continuity and Diversity* (pp. 399-417). Newton, MA: Education Development Center, Inc.

Do entire article

# of Divorce,
mployment,
Social Support
on Toddlers' Home Environments

Julie A. Poehlmann
Barbara H. Fiese

SUMMARY. The present study investigated the home environments of 45 toddlers aged 18 to 41 months whose mothers were married or divorced and working or nonworking. Stimulation in the home was evaluated with the HOME, toddler's cognitive competence was assessed using the Bayley and Stanford-Binet scales, and maternal social support was measured with the Inventory of Parent Experiences. Results indicated that divorced mothers provided their toddlers with less stimulation in the home and reported less intimate support and less satisfaction with their life situation than married mothers. Working mothers were more accepting of their child's behavior than nonworking mothers. Marital status, maternal education, and mothers' life satisfaction accounted for 43% of the variation in HOME scores, while HOME scores accounted for 11% of the variation in cognitive development scores. The need for comprehensive studies of infants and toddlers in divorced families is discussed.

Julie A. Poehlmann, MS, completed this research as part of her MS degree from the Department of Psychology, and Barbara H. Fiese, PhD, is on the faculty, Department of Psychology, Syracuse University, Syracuse, NY 13244.

Portions of this research were presented at the biennial meeting of the Society for Research in Child Development, Seattle, April 1991.

[Haworth co-indexing entry note]: "The Effects of Divorce, Maternal Employment, and Maternal Social Support on Toddlers' Home Environments." Poehlmann, Julie A., and Barbara H. Fiese. Co-published simultaneously in the *Journal of Divorce & Remarriage* (The Haworth Press, Inc.) Vol. 22, No. 1/2, 1994, pp. 121-135; and: *The Economics of Divorce: The Effects on Parents and Children* (ed: Craig A. Everett) The Haworth Press, Inc., 1994, pp. 121-135. Multiple copies of this article/chapter may be purchased from The Haworth Document Delivery Center [1-800-3-HAWORTH; 9:00 a.m. - 5:00 p.m. (EST)].

Estimates indicate that 30% to 40% of children born since 1970 will experience parental divorce by the time they are 16 years old; for almost half of these children, the divorce occurs within their first three years of life (Bumpass & Rindfuss, 1979). Although differences between married and divorced families and their preschool and schoolage children have been fairly consistently documented by the longitudinal studies of Hetherington (1989), Block and Block (Block, Block & Gjerde, 1988), and Wallerstein (Wallerstein & Blakeslee, 1989), little is known about the effects of divorce on infants and toddlers (Hetherington, Stanley-Hagen & Anderson, 1989). Because children's competencies, levels of understanding, and abilities to adjust vary with age, generalizations about older children and their surroundings may not apply to very young children. Thus, more attention should be devoted to infants and toddlers in the divorce literature.

Due to the inherent dependence of infants and toddlers on their families and to their limited experience outside of the home, the quality of a child's home environment, including experiences with caregivers, may be the most important context for early social and cognitive development (e.g., Ainsworth, Blehar, Waters & Wall, 1978; Hetherington et al., 1989). Appropriate levels of stimulation and parental accessibility and responsivity in the home have shown consistent relations to children's development, including child behavior problems (Erickson, Sroufe & Egeland, 1985), security of infant-mother attachment (Ainsworth et al., 1978; Kopera, Jacobson & Morris, 1989), and cognitive development (Gottfried & Gottfried, 1984). Furthermore, direct assessments of a child's home environment provide an ecologically valid index of the quality of early stimulation typically available to the child and of the frequency and quality of parent-child interactions, which may not be true for laboratory based studies. Because of these factors, home observations of toddlers in separated and divorced families may be particularly important to help begin to fill the void of information pertaining to toddlers in divorced families.

One of the more widely used and reliable indices of early social and cognitive stimulation in the home is Caldwell and Bradley's HOME scale (1984; Home Observation for Measurement of the Environment). The HOME has been shown to be a remarkably good indicator of later cognitive competence. For example, in a collaborative longitudinal study by Bradley et al. (1989), low HOME scores were associated with decreasing mental test profiles, while high HOME scores were generally associated with gains in mental test scores for children from a variety of social, ethnic, and geographic backgrounds.

The preschool version of the HOME has been used to assess differences in the quality of stimulation available to children in divorced and married families. Karr and Easley (1986) found that the total HOME scores of divorced families were significantly lower than those of married families. In a study that compared the home environments of married/working, married/nonworking, and divorced/working mothers, MacKinnon, Brody, and Stoneman (1982) found that married mothers provided their preschoolers with more toys, games, reading materials, and more language and academic stimulation than divorced mothers. In addition, married mothers displayed higher levels of affection and warmth to their preschoolers than divorced mothers, and many of these differences were present eighteen months later (MacKinnon et al., 1986).

MacKinnon et al. (1982, 1986) hypothesize that the disparities in available stimulation in the home may account for some of the differences found in the intelligence test performance of children from divorced and married families. In their nationwide study of divorce and child adjustment, Guidubaldi, Perry, and Cleminshaw (1984) found that first, third and fifth graders from divorced families had lower full-scale WISC-R IQ scores and lower WRAT reading, spelling, and math scores than students from married families, in addition to social and behavioral differences. Because early cognitive and social stimulation in the home may provide children with the foundations for later cognitive and social competence, it appears important to examine the early environments of children from divorced families. However, divorced families with toddlers represent a heterogenous group and may be characterized by additional factors associated with social and cognitive development during the toddler period, such as whether the mother is employed and whether adequate social supports are available to the mother.

Aside from the potentially adverse effects of parental divorce, maternal employment may have different positive and/or negative consequences for young children's development. The consideration of the effects of maternal employment on toddler's development may be particularly important in divorced families because divorced mothers obtain primary physical custody of their children in the majority of cases, especially when the child is very young (Bumpass & Rindfuss, 1979). Consequently, many divorced mothers become head of the household and find that they must seek employment outside of the home in order to maintain their standard of living. In a study that assessed the effects of early nonmaternal care (due to maternal employment) on security of infant-parent attachment, Belsky and Rovine (1988) found that infants with mothers employed over 20 hours per week were more likely to be insecurely attached than infants with mothers employed less than 20 hours per week. However, Crockenberg and Litman (1991) reported both positive and negative effects of maternal employment on maternal and toddler behavior depending on the context in which the behaviors were assessed. In their laboratory clean-up task, employed mothers were more power assertive than nonemployed mothers only when they were dissatisfied with their work role and with their social support; conversely, employed mothers used less negative control at home and were less coercive at dinnertime than nonemployed mothers (Crockenberg & Litman, 1991).

Additional studies indicate that employment status alone is not a sufficient explanation for child outcome, but that degree of satisfaction with work role and social support may be more closely related to social and cognitive development (e.g., Benn, 1986). Maternal social support has been found to have positive effects on parent and child behaviors (Jennings, Stagg & Connors, 1991; Crnic et al., 1983), including the maintenance of stimulating home environments for preschoolers (Pascoe, Loda, Jeffries & Earp, 1981). Social support may also moderate the effects of stressful circumstances, such as divorce (Caldwell & Bloom, 1982) or raising an irritable infant (Crockenberg, 1981). Therefore, in addition to considering work status of divorced families, social support should be considered in the study of social and cognitive development of toddlers raised in both divorced and married families.

The primary goal of the present study was to expand the focus of divorce research by examining families with toddlers. The quality of toddlers' home environments was assessed with the HOME inventory to determine if results with this age group replicate those of studies focusing on older children; in addition, the relation between HOME scores and cognitive competence was explored. Another goal of the study was to determine how maternal social support related to the quality of early home environments of divorced and married women, and whether amount or satisfaction with social support differed by mothers' marital or work status. The final goal of the study was to attempt to address the question of whether divorce has an impact on the home environment above and beyond that of the mother leaving the home to join the work force.

METHOD

Subjects

Participants included forty-five families with children between 18 and 41 months of age, with a mean age of 28 months. Sixteen mothers were married and nonworking (6 boys, 10 girls), 13 mothers were married and working (7 boys, 6 girls), 5 mothers were divorced and nonworking (2 boys, 3 girls), and 11 mothers were divorced and working (6 boys, 5 girls). Participants were recruited through day care centers, mother-toddler exercise groups, single parent groups, church groups, and newspaper advertisements as part of a larger study on toddler play. All of the divorced mothers and one-third of the married mothers were paid $25 for participating in the study. Paid and unpaid married mothers did not differ on any demographic variables or variables of interest in the study except maternal age; paid married mothers were somewhat older than unpaid married mothers (mean ages were 33.0 and 28.7 years, respectively).

The modal socioeconomic status (SES) of the mothers from each group was what Hollingshead (1975) terms "medium business and technical work," but ranged from semi-skilled to professional work. Mean SES scores differed by marital status (52.63 for the married group and 41.47 for the divorced group). Maternal education ranged from partial high school to graduate training, with an average of partial college or specialized training, and did not differ by marital status. The ethnic background of families was predominantly Caucasian, with only four ethnic minority participants (Hispanic and Black for the divorced group, and Asian and Oriental for the married group). There were also no differences among the groups for the demographic variables of maternal age, children's age, or number of children in the family.

The mothers in the divorced group included those women who indicated that they had been separated or divorced from their partners for at least two months. Children's age at divorce ranged from 12 months to 30 months with a mean age of 20 months. Primary physical custody of the child was with the mother in all cases. Eight (50%) of the divorced women reported that they received child support from their ex-spouse.

Instruments and Procedures

The quality of cognitive and social stimulation available to the child in the home was assessed using the infant form of Caldwell and Bradley's (1984) Home Observation for Measurement of the Environment (HOME). The HOME, which is conducted by means of a semi-structured interview and observation, was administered in the family's home when the child was awake and could be observed interacting with his or her mother. The infant version of the HOME consists of 45 items scored in a binary fashion that comprise six subscales: (1) verbal and emotional responsivity of the parent, (2) acceptance of the child, (3) organization of the temporal and physical environment, (4) provision of appropriate play materials, (5) parental involvement with the child, and (6) variety in daily stimulation. Interrater reliability for this sample was computed across 10 home observations by two independent observers and was found to be 92% for total HOME scores (averages are about 89.6% according to Elardo & Bradley, 1981). Additional psychometric data can be found in the HOME manual (Caldwell & Bradley, 1984).

Following the home interview, children's cognitive development status was assessed using the Mental Scale of the Bayley Scales for Infant Development for toddlers aged 18 to 27 months, and the Stanford-Binet (3rd edition; Terman & Merrill, 1960) for toddlers aged 28 to 41 months. MDI and IQ scores were converted to standardized scores and then pooled for the analyses.

Maternal social support was assessed by having mothers complete 33 items from Crnic et al.'s (1983) Inventory of Parent's Experiences (IPE). Three areas of support were examined for all mothers: that from friends, extended family, and intimate relationships. An additional area of support, satisfaction in the workplace, was examined for working mothers. Each of these areas involves questions about the amount of support available to the parent and the parent's satisfaction with available support; one question assesses the parent's general life satisfaction. Satisfaction with support was rated on a 4 point scale ranging from very dissatisfied (1) to very satisfied (4). The authors of the IPE provide internal consistency data on the subscales, ranging from .50 to .85, based on their sample of mothers with full-term and premature infants (Crnic et al., 1983).

Hollingshead's (1975) Four Factor Index of Social Status was used to assess families' socioeconomic status. Occupation is rated on a 9 point scale and education is rated on a 7 point scale. For married families, SES was calculated based on information about the parent(s) who worked. For divorced mothers receiving child support, SES was calculated based on information about both parents, while for divorced mothers not receiving child support, SES was calculated based on information from the mother only.

RESULTS

Due to the multiple dependent measures in the study, 2×2 (marital status $\times$ work status) multivariate analysis of variance (MANOVA) was conducted as a fairly conservative test of the hypotheses under consideration. Separate MANOVA's were performed for the HOME scales and the social support scales. Variables with significant multivariate *F*'s were subsequently analyzed using univariate analysis of variance (ANOVA).

HOME Inventory

The MANOVA executed on the HOME inventory revealed significant main effects for marital status, $F\,(3{,}39) = 5.55$, $p < .01$, and work status F (3,39) = 2.99, $p < .05$. The interaction term did not reach significance.

Seven 2 × 2 (marital status × work status) ANOVA's were performed on the total HOME score and the six HOME subscales. For the total HOME score, there was a significant main effect for marital status, F (1,41) = 15.64, $p < .001$. When the 2 items pertaining to daily involvement of the father were removed from the total HOME scores (because only the married families could receive credit for these), the main effect was still significant at the $p < .03$ level. Divorced mothers tended to provide their toddlers with less social and cognitive stimulation in the home than married mothers, regardless of their work status (means of 34.56 and 38.21, respectively, after the 2 father-involvement items were deleted). For the HOME subscales, married mothers were found to be more involved with their toddlers than divorced mothers, F (1,41) = 8.49, $p < .01$ (means of 4.86 and 3.50, respectively). The variety in daily stimulation subscale was also higher for the married group, but when the 2 father-involvement items were deleted, the effect became nonsignificant.

A significant main effect for work status was found for acceptance of the child, F (1,42) = 5.29, $p < .03$. Working mothers were more accepting of their toddler's behavior than married mothers, regardless of marital status (means of 6.83 and 6.09, respectively).

To determine whether the preceding results were due to group differences in socioeconomic status rather than family type, 2 (marital status) × 2 (work status) analysis of covariance with Hollingshead scores as the covariate were conducted on the HOME scales. Results replicated the initial analyses for all HOME data (p's $< .05$) and are represented graphically in Figure 1.

Maternal Social Support

Differences in amount of and satisfaction with social support from friends, family, and intimate relationships, as reported by mothers, were analyzed with 2 (marital status) × 2 (work status) MANOVA's. A main effect for marital status reached significance, F (3,39) = 9.82, $p < .01$, whereas the work status main effect and the interaction term did not. Follow-up univariate ANOVA's indicated that divorced mothers reported less intimate support and less satisfaction with intimate support than other mothers, F (1,41) = 12.51,

FIGURE 1. HOME total and subscale means by family form, with SES as covariate.

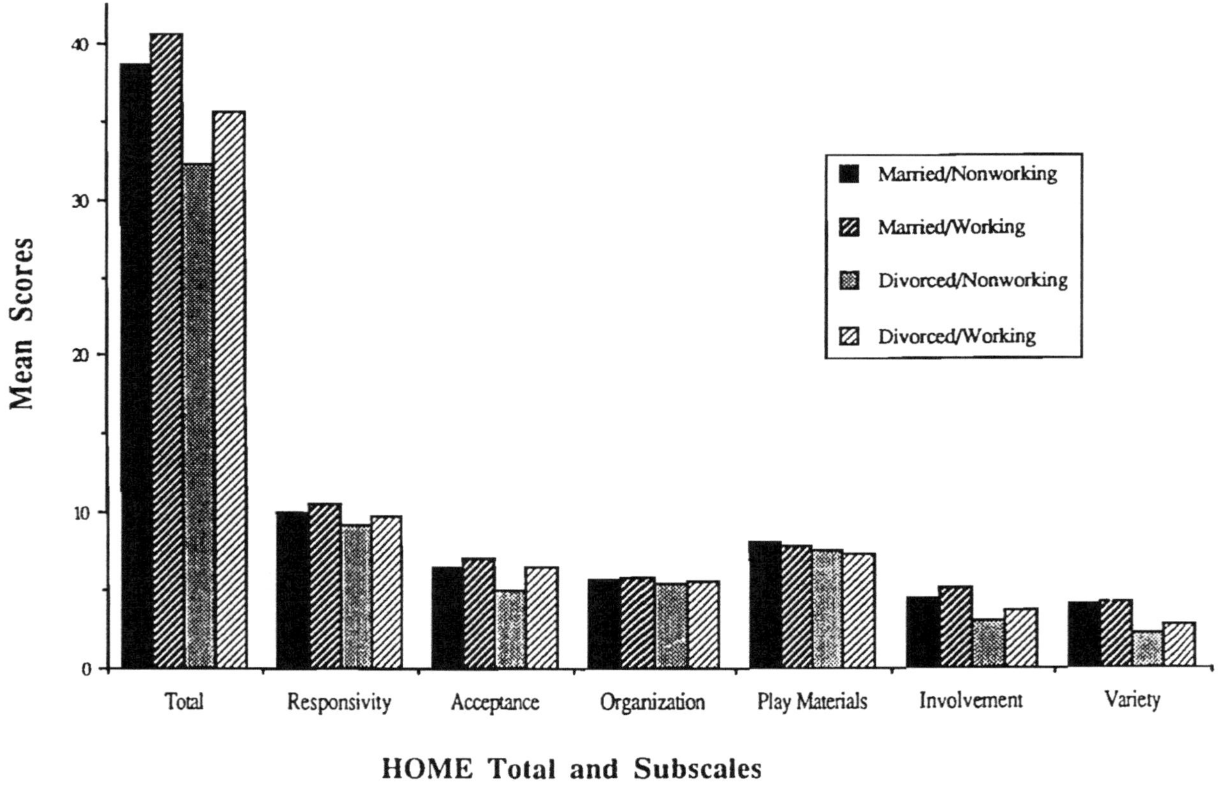

$p < .001$. Divorced mothers also reported less satisfaction with their general life situation than married mothers, $F(1,41) = 7.14, p < .02$.

Two one-way ANOVA's were performed to determine whether differences existed between married/working and divorced/working mothers regarding their satisfaction with support in the workplace. The results were nonsignificant: Working mothers reported similar satisfaction with their jobs and with support from coworkers regardless of their marital status.

Relations Among Variables

To determine the relative contributions of HOME scores and mother's marital status to toddlers' cognitive development status, hierarchical multiple regression analysis (Cohen & Cohen, 1983) was performed using IQ/MDI scores as the outcome variable. Mother's marital status was entered as the first predictor, the total HOME score was entered second, and the marital status X HOME score interaction term was entered last. Results indicated that total HOME scores alone accounted for approximately 11% of the variation in mental test scores for the total sample. The marital status and interaction terms were dropped from the model because they did not significantly increase the R^2. Maternal marital status was essentially unrelated to toddlers' mental test scores for the present sample.

Simultaneous multiple regression analysis was utilized to determine the relation of total HOME scores to maternal education and occupation, maternal social support, marital status, and mothers' work status. The criterion variable was the total HOME score and the predictor variables were maternal education level, maternal occupation level, marital status, work status, amount of social support, satisfaction with social support, and mothers' satisfaction with their general life situation. The best combination of predictors for the HOME scores across the total sample was marital status, maternal education, and general life satisfaction (see Table 1). Married, well-educated mothers who were satisfied with their life situation provided their children with the most socially and cognitively stimulating environments. These variables accounted for approximately 43% of the variation in total HOME scores.

TABLE 1. Predictor Variables and Beta Weights for Total HOME Scores.

Variables	R^2	Beta	Standard Error
	.431		
Maternal education		2.036	0.55
Marital status[1]		–2.866	1.39
General life satisfaction		0.922	0.96

[1]coded as married = 1, divorced = 2

DISCUSSION

The present study contributes to the divorce literature by empirically investigating the early environments of toddlers in divorced and married families. Social and cognitive stimulation available to children in the homes of married and divorced, working and nonworking mothers was assessed using Caldwell and Bradley's (1984) HOME inventory. Results indicated that, after statistically controlling for socioeconomic status, married mothers provided their toddlers with generally more socially and cognitively stimulating environments and were more involved with their children than divorced mothers, regardless of work status. This finding is similar to results obtained in studies comparing the early environments of preschoolers in divorced and married families (e.g., Karr & Easley, 1986; MacKinnon et al., 1982), with the exception that fewer differences between married and divorced families were found in the present sample. Perhaps if the power of the analyses in this study was greater through increased sample size, more differences would have been found. However, it is also possible that differences in divorced and married families may become more apparent as the child reaches preschool and school-age, and that the very early environments of divorced and married families are somewhat similar. This last hypothesis is quite tentative and divorced families with infants and toddlers should be examined more closely before drawing premature conclusions.

The only difference found between employed and nonemployed mothers for the present sample was that working mothers were more accepting of their toddler's behavior at home than non-working mothers. This result parallels Crockenberg and Litman's (1991) finding that maternal employment had positive effects on mothers' behavior in the home as opposed to the laboratory setting; however, it is somewhat discrepant with studies that focus on the adverse effects of maternal employment on the parenting of young children (e.g., Belsky & Rovine, 1988). Nonetheless, the results of the present study are encouraging for both divorced and married women who either choose to work or must work outside of the home to maintain their standard of living.

Divorced mothers reported similar levels of social support from friends and family but reported less intimate support and less satisfaction with intimate support than married mothers. This finding appears reasonable considering the recency of many of the mothers' divorces; it is probable that they did not yet have time to establish new intimate relationships and that the relationship with their ex-spouse was not particularly satisfying. Although divorced mothers' were as satisfied as married mothers with available social support from friends and family, they were less satisfied with their general life situations than married mothers. This difference is somewhat disheartening considering that, for the present sample, satisfaction with life situations was a more important variable in determining the quality of the home environment than was amount of or satisfaction with support from other people.

When relations among variables were examined for the entire sample, parental marital status, maternal education level, and mothers' general life satisfaction were the best predictors of total HOME scores. Divorced mothers with less education who were dissatisfied with their life situation tended to provide their toddlers with less stimulating home environments than other mothers in the study. Maternal social support variables did not increase the prediction of this model, a result that does not replicate previous findings detailing the positive effects of social support on maternal behavior (Jennings et al., 1991; Crnic et al., 1983; Crockenberg, 1981). However, the fairly strong relation between maternal education and HOME scores has been found previously. Significant relations between socioeconomic variables and HOME scores have been reported for both infants and preschoolers, with maternal education typically being one of the strongest predictors of total HOME scores (Caldwell & Bradley, 1984). Mothers with higher levels of education typically have more exposure to information about appropriate levels of social and cognitive stimulation required by young children than mothers with less education.

When relations among toddlers' cognitive development, HOME scores, and maternal marital status were examined, total HOME scores accounted for 11% of the variation in cognitive development scores, while mother's marital status was essentially unrelated to these scores. Studies that have investigated concurrent relations between infant HOME scores and Bayley or Stanford-Binet scores typically find fairly low to moderate correlations (Caldwell & Bradley, 1984); however, correlations between early HOME scores and later mental test performance tend to be substantially higher (Bradley et al., 1989; Caldwell & Bradley, 1984).

Differences on intelligence test and academic performance have been documented between children from divorced and married families (Guidubaldi et al., 1984); yet for the present sample, marital status was essentially unrelated to Bayley and Stanford-Binet scores. Because the assessments of toddlers in the present study were often conducted relatively soon after the divorce occurred and when the children were very young, it is plausible to hypothesize that differences in the relative cognitive competence of children from different family types may become more evident as children grow older and reach school-age. Furthermore, it is possible that previous studies have confounded work status and marital status when attempting to examine the effects of divorce on children.

Additional investigations of infants and toddlers in separated and divorced families are needed to adequately address these questions and discrepancies in the data. Obtaining comprehensive information about the environments and development of young children who experience parental divorce early in life may allow researchers and mental health professionals to identify points when children may be particularly vulnerable to the potentially adverse effects of marital transitions. Longitudinal data are also needed to examine the possible developmental trajectories of infants and toddlers in both divorced and married families, and to identify protective factors for young children growing up in various family environments.

REFERENCES

Ainsworth, M. D. S., Blehar, M. C., Waters, E., & Wall, S. (1978). *Patterns of attachment: A psychological study of the strange situation*. Hillsdale, NJ: Erlbaum.

Belsky, J., & Rovine, M. J. (1988). Nonmaternal care in the first year of life and the security of infant-parent attachment. *Child Development, 59*, 157-167.

Benn, R. (1986). Factors promoting secure attachment relationships between employed mothers and their sons. *Child Development, 57*, 1224-1231.

Block, J., Block, J. H., & Gjerde, P. F. (1988). Parental functioning and the home environment in families of divorce: Prospective and concurrent analyses. *Journal of the American Academy of Child and Adolescent Psychiatry, 27*, 207-213.

Bradley, R. H., Caldwell, B. M., Rock, S. L., Ramey, C. T., Barnard, K. E., Gray, C., Hammond, M. A., Mitchell, S., Gottfried, A. W., Siegel, L., & Johnson, D. L. (1989). Home environment and cognitive development in the first 3 years of life: A collaborative study involving six sites and three ethnic groups in North America. *Developmental Psychology, 22*, 723-742.

Bumpass, L., & Rindfuss, R. R. (1979). Children's experience of marital disruption. *American Journal of Sociology, 85*, 49-65.

Caldwell, B. M., & Bradley, R. H. (1984). *Home observation for measurement of the environment*. Little Rock: University of Arkansas.

Caldwell, R. A., & Bloom, B. L. (1982). Social support: Its structure and impact on marital disruption. *American Journal of Community Psychology, 10*, 647-667.

Cohen, J., & Cohen, P. (1983). *Applied regression/correlation analysis for the behavioral sciences* (2nd ed.). Hillsdale, NJ: Erlbaum.

Crnic, K. A., Greenberg, M. T., Ragozin, A. S., Robinson, N. M., & Basham, R. B. (1983). Effects of stress and social support on mothers and premature and full-term infants. *Child Development, 54*, 209-217.

Crockenberg, S. (1981). Infant irritability, mother responsiveness, and social support influences on the security of infant-mother attachment. *Child Development, 52*, 857-865.

Crockenberg, S., & Litman, C. (1991). Effects of maternal employment on maternal and two-year-old child behavior. *Child Development, 62*, 930-953.

Elardo, R., & Bradley, R. H. (1981). The Home Observation for Measurement of the Environment (HOME) Scale: A review of the research. *Developmental Review, 1*, 113-145.

Erickson, M. F., Sroufe, L. A., & Egeland, B. (1985). The relationship between quality of attachment and behavior problems in preschool in a high-risk sample. *Monographs of the Society for Research in Child Development, 50*, (1-2, Serial No. 209).

Gottfried, A. W., & Gottfried, A. E. (1984). Home environment and cognitive development in young children of middle-socioeconomic-status families. In A.

W. Gottfried (Ed.), *Home environment and early cognitive development: Longitudinal research* (pp. 57-115). New York: Academic Press.
Guidubaldi, J., Perry, J. D., & Cleminshaw, H. K. (1984). The legacy of parental divorce: A nationwide study of family status and selected mediating variables on children's academic and social competencies. In B. B. Lahey and A. E. Kazdin (Eds.), *Advances in Clinical Child Psychology, Vol. 7* (pp. 109-151). New York: Plenum Press.
Hetherington, E. M. (1989). Coping with family transitions: Winners, losers, and survivors. *Child Development, 60*, 1-14.
Hetherington, E. M., Stanley-Hagen, M., & Anderson, E. R. (1989). Marital transitions: A child's perspective. *American Psychologist, 44*, 303-312.
Hollingshead, A. B. (1975). *Four factor index of social status*. Unpublished manuscript, Yale University, Department of Sociology, New Haven.
Jennings, K. D., Stagg, V., & Connors, R. E. (1991). Social networks and mothers' interactions with their preschool children. *Child Development, 62*, 966-978.
Karr, S. K., & Easley, B. (1986). Exploration of effects of divorce on the preschool home inventory. *Psychological Reports, 59*, 659-662.
Kopera, K. F., Jacobson, W. W., & Morris, C. (April, 1989). The influence of perceived social support, maternal affect and the HOME on attachment. Paper presented at the biennial meeting of the Society for Research in Child Development, Kansas City, MO.
MacKinnon, C. E., Brody, G. H., & Stoneman, Z. (1982). The effects of divorce and maternal employment on the home environments of preschool children. *Child Development, 53*, 1392-1399.
MacKinnon, C. E., Brody, G. H., & Stoneman, Z. (1986). The longitudinal effects of divorce and maternal employment on the home environments of preschool children. *Journal of Divorce, 9*, 65-78.
Pascoe, J. M., Loda, F. A., Jeffries, F., & Earp, J. A. (1981). The association between mothers' social support and provision of stimulation to their children. *Journal of Developmental and Behavioral Pediatrics, 2*, 15-19.
Terman, L. M., & Merrill, M. A. (1960). *Stanford-Binet Intelligence Scale: Manual for the third revision, Form L-M*. Boston: Houghton Mifflin.
Wallerstein, J. S., & Blakeslee, S. (1989). *Second chances: Men, women, and children a decade after divorce*. New York: Ticknor & Fields.

Do This
Whole
Article

Family Configuration and Maternal Employment: Effects on Family Environment and Children's Outcomes

Linda Kurtz
Jeffrey L. Derevensky

SUMMARY. The purpose of this study was to investigate the effects of maternal employment on children's outcomes and the social climate within divorced (N = 38) and intact (N = 38) middle class families having elementary school children. Parental perceptions of specific family environment characteristics (Moos & Moos, 1986) and children's behavioral conduct (Achenbach & Edelbrock, 1983) were assessed. Children's outcome characteristics were measured using the Harter Self Perception Profile For Children (Harter, 1985). These data were analyzed using a multiple regression model. As

---

Linda Kurtz, RN, MA, completed this research as part of her graduate program and Jeffrey L. Derevensky, PhD, is Associate Professor, Department of Educational Psychology and Counselling, McGill University, Montreal, Canada.

This is a revision of a paper presented at the Canadian Psychological Association Annual Convention, Quebec City, June, 1992. Research was supported by the Social Sciences and Humanities Research Council of Canada. Special thanks to George M. Tarabulsy M.A. (Laval University, Quebec, Canada) for his participation in this project.

Correspondence should be addressed to the authors, McGill University, Educational Psychology and Counseling Department, 3700 McTavish Street, Montreal, Quebec, Canada, H3A 1Y2.

[Haworth co-indexing entry note]: "Family Configuration and Maternal Employment: Effects on Family Environment and Children's Outcomes." Kurtz, Linda, and Jeffrey L. Derevensky. Co-published simultaneously in the *Journal of Divorce & Remarriage* (The Haworth Press, Inc.) Vol. 22, No. 1/2, 1994, pp. 137-154; and: *The Economics of Divorce: The Effects on Parents and Children* (ed: Craig A. Everett) The Haworth Press, Inc., 1994, pp. 137-154. Multiple copies of this article/chapter may be purchased from The Haworth Document Delivery Center [1-800-3-HAWORTH; 9:00 a.m. - 5:00 p.m. (EST)].

expected, significantly more mothers were employed in the divorced group. In divorced homes, maternal employment was significantly associated with increased active recreational orientation within the family environment and increased self-esteem in children. The data suggest that when mothers are employed in families who have experienced parental divorce, there is more of an inclination to participate in social and recreational activities together. Children within this category expressed elevated global evaluations of self-worth. Interestingly, a significant negative relationship was observed between maternal employment and duration of visitation with the child by the noncustodial parent. Maternal employment in intact families was found to be associated with decreased emphasis on independence within the family environment and increased athletic self-efficacy in children. No significant differences were observed between dual-wage and single-wage families in terms of parental reports of children's behavioral profiles, regardless of family configuration. This research supports the contention that the relationship between recent societal changes and children's outcomes are mediated by specific family process variables.

The structure of the North American family has undergone significant changes in the past three decades. The incidence of families involved in marital dissolution remains at record levels, with an estimated 70 percent of all divorces involving children (Block, Block, & Gjerde, 1986; 1988; Shamsie, 1985). Approximately 45 percent of children born since 1970 will experience an average of six childhood years in a single parent home, usually headed by the mother, as a consequence of divorce (Hetherington, Stanley-Hagan, & Anderson, 1989). The majority of divorced individuals remarry within two to five years, nevertheless, the divorce rate remains comparatively higher for second marriages. Given the multitude of developmental changes, the occurrence of divorce and remarriage must be understood as a process, rather than an isolated event, which significantly impacts upon the development of children.

Concomitant with these statistics, the impact of divorce on children has increasingly become a topic of concern in developmental research. The nature and course of adaptation following divorce has been shown to vary, often dependent upon the child's age, sex, temperament, and a host of other psychosocial factors (Tschann, Johnston, Kline, & Wallerstein, 1989). In fact, children at different developmental levels have been shown to exhibit variability in their coping strategies and specific social and cognitive competencies, making postdivorce adjustment qualitatively distinct (Kurtz & Derevensky, in press; Tarabulsy & Derevensky, 1990a; Tarabulsy & Derevensky, 1990b; Tarabulsy, Kurtz, & Derevensky, 1991).

The experience of parental divorce involves a high level of interparental conflict before, during, and after parental separation itself. Although the experience of divorce and continuous interparental conflict places all family members at risk for psychological difficulty, significant associations between the divorce process and child outcomes have been reported in the literature. Short and long term consequences of parental divorce have been well documented.

Three consistent findings have surfaced in two seminal longitudinal studies (Hetherington, 1989; Hetherington et al., 1989; Wallerstein & Blakeslee, 1989; Wallerstein & Kelly, 1980). First, children invariably experience short term adverse effects in postdivorce adjustment, regardless of age. Poor academic performance, low self-esteem, problems in peer relationships, and difficulties in emotional well-being are not uncommon. Following the acute responses observed during the crisis period, more than half of children who have experienced parental divorce appear remarkably resilient and may actually develop enhanced coping mechanisms over the long term. Second, the exact nature and course of postdivorce adjustment varies according to a number of important factors, namely, developmental level, sex, birth order, dependency on parents, and social and cognitive competencies (Derevensky & Tarabulsy, 1991; Kurtz, Tarabulsy, Derevensky, & Lo, 1991). Third, long term adverse effects have been documented in over one-third of children who have experienced parental divorce, with childhood depression being the most frequent clinical diagnosis five years after the breakup. An increased frequency of conduct and behavioral disorders has been reported as well (Peterson & Zill, 1986).

The literature strongly suggests that family transition in the form of parental separation, divorce, and remarriage often interrupts the emotional, social, and academic/occupational development of the children involved (Forehand, McCombs Thomas, Wierson, Brody, & Fauber, 1990; Hetherington, 1989; Kurtz & Derevensky, in press). That is, most parents and children adapt to the changes brought on by the divorce within two to three years, provided that the situation is not complicated by additional demands for transition. However, the custodial parent is likely to remarry during the postdivorce period, compounding the family situation with what is perceived by children as additional adversity. Hence, the term *family disruption* descriptively encompasses the most deleterious effects of families undergoing transition.

A parent's decision to divorce is often pursued with the aim of improving the family's well-being (Hetherington et al., 1989). Unfortunately, the consequences are often negative for the children involved, and the benefits for the adult are mostly felt over the long term (Wallerstein & Blakeslee, 1989; Wallerstein & Kelly, 1980). A child's psychological vulnerability is often increased by the functional absence of a parent and a disrupted relationship with a custodial parent who is frequently overburdened with responsibilities and emotionally overtaxed.

In addition to this disequilibrium, family transition is complicated by the restructuring of living arrangements, with additional changes in family lifestyles, rules, and relationships. Parental separation and divorce is significantly associated with a steep decline in income, especially for households in which mothers retain physical custody (Hernandez, 1988). This marked lack of income is partly attributable to husbands who are noncompliant with child support arrangements and to the inability for women in this situation to meet the requirements of well paying jobs (Hetherington, 1989; Hetherington & Camara, 1984). Reduced economics following divorce are often associated with a series of concomitants, one being a sudden necessity for maternal employment.

MATERNAL EMPLOYMENT

Maternal employment has become a common family characteristic in North America. The most significant increase in maternal employment has been for families with infants and preschoolers, a rate which has doubled in the United States since 1970 (Clarke-Stewart, 1989; Hoffman, 1989). Recent research has given considerable attention to the effects of maternal employment on younger children's outcomes in the two parent family. Fewer studies have directly addressed the issue of maternal employment in homes experiencing family transition (Kurtz & Derevensky, 1992).

Nevertheless, the dual-wage intact family has been the major focus of study. The results of such investigations appear nebulous due to methodological difficulties, rendering maternal employment, per se, not as robust a variable. Researchers have come to conclude that the relationship between maternal employment and children's outcomes appears to be mediated by certain intervening processes.

Previous studies from the 1960s and 1970s employed designs that involved comparisons between school-aged children from homes with mothers who were currently employed, with children from homes with full-time homemakers. Moreover, whether work was part-time or full-time was frequently not specified. Notwithstanding such limitations, a pattern of diminished sex-role traditionalism among children from families with maternal employment, an increased parental focus on children's independence training, and decreased school performance among middle class sons was found (Hoffman, 1979).

Investigations conducted in the 1980s have confirmed the pattern of diminished sex-role traditionalism and increased children's independence training in children from dual-wage intact homes. However, a decrement in cognitive performance among middle class sons has not been corroborated (Hoffman, 1989). The current research is distinct in that it focuses on the younger child and greater attention is given to the family process variables thought to moderate the effects on children's adjustment. Moreover, investigators do not appear unified in their position on this topic, as two conflicting perspectives exist in the literature. The first positively views maternal employment as a morale booster while the second takes a negative perspective of it as a stressor. Both points of view have acquired support, however, it appears that maternal employment becomes stressful in a select population of individuals who often lack social support (i.e., instrumental, empathetic, physical) resources. Subsequent to divorce, custodial mothers often fall in this category.

In general, current studies have examined the effects on the parents, marital relationship, parent-child interaction, and children's outcomes. The results suggest that employed mothers have three major concerns (Hoffman, 1989): (1) worries about insufficient time for the family, individual children, and tasks; (2) whether their work is placing their children at a disadvantage; and (3) constant concern about finding adequate child-care arrangements. The effects of maternal employment on the father are mediated by social class, the parents' sex role attitudes, and the degree of paternal participation in household and child-care tasks (Kessler & McRae, 1982). More specifically, maternal employment is negatively associated with the father's overall satisfaction in the blue collar class, where traditional sex-role ideologies are frequently found. Some findings suggest that this may explain why a strain in the father-son relationship has often been observed (Hoffman, 1979). Increased paternal involvement in household and child-care tasks appears to have positive effects on the father's self-esteem and family members in general. However, maternal employment has been related to interparental conflict when the father is not intrinsically motivated to engage in household related chores, especially in blue collar samples. When parental attitudes and commitment to parenting are considered as co-variates, few differences have been noted between dual-wage and single-wage families. Albeit, mothers who are employed full-time do spend less time with their younger children, they tend to make up this difference in family time on weekends (Hoffman, 1984). Moreover, the parent-child interaction findings indicate that there is a greater focus on independence training and a *possible* preference for girls (Hoffman, 1979). Hoffman contends that greater emphasis on independence training may benefit daughters in terms of role modeling and organization skills, however, the advantages for sons remain ambiguous.

Several studies have considered specific aspects of maternal employment. Working more than 40 hours a week has been deemed detrimental to children's development (Hoffman, 1989). When compared to full-time work and full-time homemaking, part-time employment has been associated with more positive outcomes for family life and children's development (Hoffman, 1984). Lastly, some questions about timing upon return to work have been asked. For example, a return to work during a period of family transition has been found to be disruptive to younger children (Hoffman, 1981). Whether a return to work in early infancy is more or less disruptive than a return to work in later infancy has been examined as well (Goldberg & Easterbrooks, 1988). However, the findings are not yet consolidated to provide a conclusive answer (Hoffman, 1989).

Although the dual-wage parental unit in North America is the modal family style of the 21st century, it continues to be a significant challenge in homes with families in transition. In addition, the benefits of maternal employment have been obstructed by society's poor acceptance of change, consequently resulting in limited social support for the working mother in the form of instrumental, empathic, and physical assistance (Hoffman, 1989). It is anticipated that as social attitudes and public policy become congruent with the prevailing family state, conditions promoting adaptation in all family members will likely increase.

The purpose of this study was to investigate the effects of maternal employment on children's outcomes and the family social climate within divorced and intact families. Parental perceptions of specific family environment characteristics and children's behavioral conduct were comparatively assessed. With respect to children's outcome characteristics, self-esteem and perceived self-efficacy were focussed upon.

METHOD

Subjects

Seventy-six elementary school children attending one of five English elementary schools and their parents participated in this study. This sample consisted of 40 girls (52.6%) and 36 boys (47.4%). The average age was 9.1 years, with an age range of six to 13 years (s.d. = 1.6). Children were selected from a voluntary sample of 359 middle class families living in a suburban area of Montreal. Half of the children were from homes where parental divorce had occurred and the remaining children were from homes with no previous history of parental separation. To achieve an equal number of subjects, children from consenting intact families were randomly selected for participation. All children had an average of one sibling. Only custodial parents were requested to participate in the divorced group.

The Divorced Group

The divorced group consisted of 18 boys (47.4%) and 20 girls (52.6%), with an average 9.1 years of age, with an age range of six to 12 and a standard deviation of 1.7. Their biological parents had been legally divorced for an average of 4.4 years, with the time since divorce ranging from 1 month to 10.4 years (s.d. = 3.3 years). In this particular sample, all cases of parental separation resulted in legal divorce. One child had experienced two parental divorces. Maternal custody was in effect for 82% of the families. Six custodial parents (15.8%) were presently remarried. Their inclusion in the divorced group was justified by the fact that the children involved had experienced the disruption of their biological parents. This subgroup was not found to differ from the experimental group in terms of the variables examined in the present study. Moreover, Hetherington (1989) has suggested that children from homes that have undergone divorce and remarriage experience similar degrees of family disruption, as both are forms of family transition and consequently involve the reorganization of the family and household.

The Intact Group

The intact group consisted of 18 boys and 20 girls. The average age was 9.1 years, with a range of seven to 13 years and a standard deviation of 1.5 years.

Measures

Perceived Competence Scale for Children (Harter, 1985) [HSPP]

The HSPP, a 36-item self report instrument, was used to measure self-efficacy. It is designed to assess a child's self perceived competence in six different areas of functioning (cognitive, athletic, social, behavioral, physical appearance, and global self worth). This scale has two forms, an individually administered pictorial version for children aged four to seven, and a Likert-type scale appropriate for children aged eight to 14. These versions yield overlapping subscale scores in cognitive, social, and athletic perceived self competence, as well as a general self worth score. In the present study, self-esteem, and cognitive, social, behavioral and athletic perceived self-efficacy were of interest. Factorial validity has consistently confirmed six subscales for the HSPP, with internal consistency varying from .73 to .86 across all domains. Test-retest reliability ranges from .69 to .87 (Harter & Pike, 1984).

Child Behavior Checklist (Achenbach & Edelbrock, 1983) [CBCL]

The CBCL is a 118 item parent report that is appropriate for children aged four to 16. The CBCL reports parental views of the child's social competence, behavior problems, and symptom array on a three point scale. It yields T scores and subscores which control for gender and age differences in behavior problems. Items are scored on a number of narrow band or two broad band scales. For the present study, the broad band scales labeled internalizing and externalizing were used. The CBCL has substantial reliability (test/retest reliability −.84) and adequately discriminates between clinical and nonclinical populations.

The Family Environment Scale (Moos & Moos, 1986) [FES]

The FES (Form R) is a 90 item true/false instrument that assesses family social climate. It consists of ten subscales which provide information on relationship, personal growth, and system maintenance dimensions within the family. The relationship dimension is measured by the cohesion, expressiveness, and conflict subscales. The personal growth dimension includes the independence, achievement orientation, intellectual-cultural orientation, active-recreational orientation and moral-religious emphasis subscales. The system maintenance dimension is comprised of the organization, and control subscales. Seven subscales were focussed upon in this investigation (Cohesion, Expressiveness, Independence, Intellectual-Cultural Orientation, Organization, Active-Recreational Orientation, Control). The FES has adequate construct validity and reliability (test/retest reliability ranging from .68 to .86 at an eight week interval).

Design and Procedure

The present study took place in the context of a larger project. The differences between family social climate variables, behavior and self-referent thought in children from maternally employed homes and homes without maternal employment were examined in both the divorced and intact groups, respectively. Within-group relationships were examined using a quasi-experimental design. A previous study (Kurtz & Derevensky, in press) conducted a between-groups investigation and found significantly less cohesion in the family social climate of divorced homes. Moreover, no differences were observed between divorced and intact families with respect to conflict levels within the home and children's behavioral profiles.

Children in grades one through six in five elementary schools were selected based upon parental willingness to participate. The HSPP self report was group administered to small groups of children in grades two to six. Younger children (grade one) were individually administered the HPCSA pictorial version. The Harter scales were completed by children with an average testing time of twenty minutes.

Parents were sent a package containing the CBCL and FES with an instructional cover letter requesting them to complete the scales. It was estimated that the total testing time for completion of both scales by parents was 30 minutes. More intact families consented to participate (321 intact families versus 38 divorced families), as has often been the case in previous studies. All test protocols were scored according to their accompanying manuals.

RESULTS

A stepwise multiple regression model was employed to assess the influence of maternal employment on family social climate, parental perceptions of children's behavior, and children's self referent thought (self-esteem and self-efficacy) in intact and divorced families. Descriptive statistics for both groups are shown in Table 1. Dummy coding was used to enter maternal employment as a dichotomous dependent variable for both groups. The two groups differed in maternal employment, as the divorced group reported significantly greater maternal employment [$t(74) = 2.54$, $p < .01$]. This observation was not surprising since it is consistent with previous findings indicating the necessity for greater maternal employment in order to attenuate the diminished financial standard of living subsequent to divorce (Colletta, 1979; Wallerstein & Blakeslee, 1989; Weiss, 1979).

In the sample of divorced families, the FES Active Recreational Organization Subscale was found to be a significant predictor of maternal employment [$F(7, 25) = 4.52$, $p < .05$]. There was no significant relationship between maternal employment status and parental perceptions of children's behavior. However, a significant positive association between children's estimates of global self-worth (i.e., self-esteem) and maternal employment was observed in this group [$F(4, 29) = 4.26$, $p < .05$]. Interestingly, duration of visitation with the child by the noncustodial parent was found to be a negative predictor of maternal employment [$F(2, 35) = 4.88$, $p < .05$].

In the sample of intact families, FES Independence subscale was negatively associated with maternal employment [$FES(7, 22) = 5.08$, $p < .05$]. Children's perceived self-efficacy in the athletic domain was found to be a positive predictor of maternal employment status [$F(6, 28) = 5.97$, $p < .05$]. Children's global estimates of self-worth were not observed to be significantly related to maternal occupational status. As in the divorced group, parental perceptions of children's behavior, as measured by the CBCL, were not found to be related to maternal employment status.

DISCUSSION

The hypothesis that family environment and children's characteristics in the two family configurations would differ in relation to maternal employment was supported. As expected, significantly

TABLE 1: Descriptive statistics of children's self referent thought, parental perceptions of children's behavior, and family social climate for divorced (n = 38) and intact families (n = 38) based upon maternal employment status.

Variable	Divorced No Mat. Employ. Mean (S.D.)	Divorced Yes Mat. Employ. Mean (S.D.)	Intact No Mat. Employ. Mean (S.D.)	Intact Yes Mat. Employ. Mean (S.D.)
HSPP				
Cognitive Self-Eff.	14.3 (2.7)	16.3 (4.3)	19.3 (3.0)	18.5 (4.1)
Social Self-Eff.	16.7 (3.6)	16.8 (4.8)	17.1 (4.0)	17.4 (3.9)
Athletic Self-Eff.	16.0 (4.6)	18.1 (4.0)	16.1 (4.3)	18.5 (4.0)
Behavioral Self-Eff.	15.2 (3.8)	17.1 (4.5)	19.4 (3.1)	18.5 (2.9)
Self-Esteem	13.8 (3.5)	17.6 (4.2)	18.7 (3.6)	18.1 (4.0)
CBCL				
Internalizing	15.0 (5.2)	12.7 (9.3)	8.1 (5.5)	9.9 (6.6)
Externalizing	21.8 (8.9)	15.6 (11.1)	10.7 (8.2)	13.0 (11.5)
FES				
Cohesion	7.4 (1.6)	7.6 (1.1)	8.3 (0.7)	7.5 (1.3)
Expressiveness	5.5 (1.6)	6.6 (1.2)	6.2 (2.0)	6.4 (1.6)
Independence	5.5 (1.1)	6.4 (0.7)	6.6 (0.9)	5.7 (1.4)
Int. Cult. Orientation	5.7 (1.9)	6.0 (1.6)	6.5 (2.3)	6.1 (2.0)
Act. Rec. Orientation	3.2 (2.2)	5.9 (1.9)	6.6 (1.5)	6.5 (1.9)
Organizational	5.8 (2.1)	6.7 (1.9)	6.1 (2.1)	5.6 (2.1)
Control	5.0 (2.4)	5.4 (1.6)	4.7 (1.8)	4.6 (2.0)

more mothers were employed in the divorced group. The contention that the relationship between maternal employment and children's outcomes is moderated by specific family process variables was supported by these data.

In *divorced* homes, maternal employment was significantly associated with increased active recreational orientation within the family environment and increased self-esteem in children. The data suggest that when mothers are employed in homes that have experienced parental divorce, there is more of an inclination to participate in social and recreational activities together. Interestingly, investigations of the parent-child relationship in maternally employed dual-wage families have found that mothers tend to compensate for their absence during work hours by an increased proportion in direct interaction and in the amount of time spent with the child during nonwork hours (i.e., evenings and weekends) (Easterbrooks & Goldberg, 1985; Hoffman, 1984). Perhaps such compensation is intentionally augmented in divorced homes where the custodial parent, frequently the mother, is employed because she has increased total time with the children (in comparison with the noncustodial parent) and may perceive herself as the psychological parent because of her custodial status. This explanation is very plausible considering the fact that sole maternal custody was in effect for the preponderance of the sample used in this study.

Children within this category expressed elevated global evaluations of self-worth. More specifically, children from divorced families with mothers who were employed were more likely to report increased self-esteem than children from divorced families being raised by full-time homemakers. This finding may be explained by a multitude of factors. First, maternally employed divorced families may be comparatively better off socioeconomically than their nonmaternally employed counterparts, maximizing opportunities for the children involved to participate in extracurricular activities which require funding. Secondly, Weinraub, Jaeger, and Hoffman (1988) found that children from dual-wage families in which mothers worked outside the home were reared with greater stress on independence training. It can be speculated that perhaps this is even more evident in divorced homes with employed mothers, resulting in comparatively more independent children. On the one hand, it is reasonable to expect that such an increase in self-sufficiency may be related to a boost in children's self-esteem. On the other hand, previous research has characterized children of divorce as "hurried children" (Elkind, 1981; Weiss, 1979). However, these results suggest that this may have been an overgeneralization, especially when mediating factors such as the effects of maternal employment on the family system are considered. Lastly, it is likely that children's augmented evaluations of global self-worth may simply be the result of an increased active recreational orientation within the family environment of the divorced home, as was observed.

Interestingly, a significant negative relationship was found between maternal employment and duration of visitation with the child by the noncustodial parent. That total access time for the noncustodial parent was decreased in families where the mother worked outside the home was not surprising. Specifically, mothers may require the extra hours for the purpose of compensation in quality time, thus impinging upon duration of noncustodial (paternal in this sample) visitation.

Maternal employment in *intact* families was significantly associated with decreased emphasis on independence within the family environment and increased athletic self-efficacy in children. The finding with respect to more dependency being promoted in the intact family environment tends to logically concur with the literature demonstrating an increased emphasis upon independence in intact dual-wage families (Weinraub et al., 1988). Homes with working mothers require fathers and children to participate in household responsibility because of necessity and not just changing societal roles (Pleck, 1983). It is possible that women who choose to become full-time homemakers may be more willing to assume traditional roles to validate their occupational status in a society where they are the minority. There is also comparatively less temporal pressure in completing household chores. Hence, these findings concur with the literature that indicates that children are likely to be less independent in single-wage intact homes.

This investigation examined two aspects of children's outcome variables, their self referent thought and parental perceptions of behavior. Although there were no differences in children's behavior between and within groups, within-group differences were detected in children's self referent thought. In children who have experienced parental divorce, differences in self-esteem were observed, with maternal employment serving as the mediating variable. Similarly, within-group differences in self-efficacy were found in children from intact families, depending on whether they were from single-wage or dual-wage families. These two constructs differ in that self-efficacy pertains to judgements of personal capabilities that vary across situations, whereas, self-esteem pertains to overall self-worth. Hence, self-efficacy can be conceptualized as a judgement of context specific ability rather than a global self-evaluation of worthiness (Bandura, 1986).

The relationship between maternal employment status and its influence on child adjustment is mediated by the mother's personal preference to work and her emotional state (Hoffman, 1989). The literature presents two seemingly incongruent perspectives of the effects of maternal employment upon children. One is that maternal employment can enhance a woman's life, and the other views the roles of mother and worker as a double bind. Although the state of maternal adaptation to her situation was not explored in this study, studies indicate that maternal employment is more likely to be perceived as a negative stressor in families in transition, as it is pursued because of economic need rather than personal preference (Hetherington & Camara, 1984).

With respect to child-care following divorce, joint custody is rapidly becoming a very common postdivorce arrangement in North America. In fact, there is a strong push for a rebuttable presumption making shared parenting the preferred legal disposition in custody disputes (Fidler, Saunders, Freedman & Hood, 1989; Sorenson & Goldman, 1990). Such a new family form may have implications for patterns in parental employment and the economic needs of the family. Future research addressing maternal employment patterns within differing custody determinations is warranted.

This research represents an investigation of two recent major changes in society that have implications for the family and its socio-emotional environment. *Maternal employment* and the *changing structure* of the North American family appear to be relatively permanent states influencing adjustment in its members and child-rearing patterns. In order to more fully comprehend their concomitant processes, these two variables must be examined in concert.

REFERENCES

Achenbach, T.M., & Edelbrock, C.S. (1983). *Manual for the child behavior checklist and revised child behavior profile.* Burlington, VT: Dept. of Psychiatry at the University of Vermont.

Bandura, A. (1986). *Social foundations of thought and action: A social-cognitive theory.* Englewood Cliffs, NJ: Prentice Hall.

Block, J.H., Block, J., & Gjerde, P.F. (1986). The personality of children prior to divorce. *Child Development, 57*, 827-840.

Block, J.H., Block, J., & Gjerde, P.F. (1988). Parental functioning and the home environment in families of divorce: Prospective and concurrent analysis. *Journal of American Academy of Child and Adolescent Psychiatry, 27(2)*, 207-213.

Clark-Stewart, K.A. (1989). Infant day care: Maligned or Malignant? *American Psychologist, 44*, 266-273.

Colletta, N.D. (1979). The impact of divorce: Father absence or poverty? *Journal of Divorce, 3*, 27-36.

Derevensky, J.L., & Tarabulsy, G.M. (April, 1991). *An empirical examination of the applications of stress-coping theory for children from divorced homes.* Paper presented at the Society for Research in Child Development Conference, Seattle.

Easterbrooks, M.A., & Goldberg, W.A. (1985). Effects of early maternal employment on toddlers, mothers, and fathers. *Developmental Psychology, 4*, 774-783.

Elkind, D. (1981). *The hurried child: Growing up too fast, too soon.* Massachusetts: Addison-Wesley.

Fidler, B.J., Saunders, E., Freedman, E., & Hood, E. (1989). Joint custody: Historical, legal, and clinical perspectives with emphasis on the situation in Canada. *Canadian Journal of Psychiatry, 34*, 561-568.

Forehand, R., McCombs Thomas, A., Wierson, M., Brody, G., & Fauber, R. (1990). Role of maternal functioning and parenting skills in adolescent functioning following parental divorce. *Journal of Abnormal Psychology, 99*(3), 278-283.

Goldberg, W.A., & Easterbrooks, M.A. (1988). Maternal employment when children and toddlers are kindergarteners. In A.E. Gottfried & A.W. Gottfried (Eds.), *Maternal employment and children's development: Longitudinal research* (pp. 121-154). New York: Plenum.

Harter, S. (1985). *Manual for the self perception profile for children.* Colorado: University of Denver.

Harter, S., & Pike, R. (1984). The pictorial scale of perceived competence and social acceptance for young children. *Child Development, 55*, 1969-1982.

Hernandez, D.J. (1988). Demographic trends and the living arrangements of children. In E.M. Hetherington & J.D. Arasteh (Eds.), *Impact of divorce, single-parenting, and step-parenting on children* (pp. 3-22). Hillsdale: Erlbaum.

Hetherington, E.M. (1989). Coping with family transition: Winners, losers, and survivors. *Child Development, 60*(1), 1-14.

Hetherington, E.M., & Camara, K.A. (1984). Families in transition: The processes of dissolution and reconstitution. In R.D. Parke (Ed.), *The family: Review of child development research* (Vol. 7, pp. 398-439). Chicago: University of Chicago Press.

Hetherington, E.M., Stanley-Hagan, & Anderson (1989). Marital transitions: A child's perspective. *American Psychologist, 44*(2), 303-312.

Hoffman, L.W. (1979). Maternal employment: 1979. *American Psychologist, 34*, 859-865.

Hoffman, L.W. (1981). *Foundations of family therapy*. New York: Basic Books.

Hoffman, L.W. (1984). Work, family, and the socialization of the child. In R.D. Parke (Ed.), *The family: Review of child development research* (Vol. 7, pp. 223-282). Chicago: University of Chicago Press.

Hoffman, L.W. (1989). Effects of maternal employment in the two parent family. *American Psychologist, 44*, 282-292.

Kessler, R.C., & McRae, J.A., Jr. (1982). The effects of wives' employment on the mental health of married men and women. *American Psychological Review, 47*, 216-227.

Kurtz, L., & Derevensky, J.L. (1992). *Adolescent motherhood: An application of the stress-coping model to child-rearing attitudes and practices*. Manuscript submitted.

Kurtz, L., & Derevensky, J.L. (in press). The effects of divorce on perceived self-efficacy and behavioral control in elementary school children. *Journal of Divorce & Remarriage. 19.*

Kurtz, L., Tarabulsy, G.M., Derevensky, J.L., & Lo, E. (1991). Self perceptions of behavioral efficacy in children of divorce. *Canadian Psychology, 32*(2), 252.

Moos, R.H., & Moos, B.S. (1986). *Family environment scale manual* (2nd Ed.). Consulting Psychologists Press, Inc.

Peterson, J.L., & Zill, N. (1986). Marital disruption, parent-child relationships, and behavior problems in children. *Journal of Marriage and the Family, 48*, 295-307.

Pleck, J.R. (1983). Husbands' paid work and family roles: Current research issues. In H.Z. Lopata & J.H. Pleck (Eds.), *Research in the interweave of social roles: Families and jobs* (pp. 251-333). Greenwich, CT: JAI Press.

Shamsie, J. (1985). Family breakdown and its effects on emotional disorders in children. *Canadian Journal of Psychiatry, 30*, 281-287.

Sorenson, E.D., & Goldman, J. (1990). Custody determinations and child development: A review of the current literature. *Journal of Divorce, 13*(4), 53-67.

Tarabulsy, G.M., & Derevensky, J.L. (1990a). Coping mechanisms and children from divorced parents. In S. Dansereau, B. Terrisse, & J.M. Bouchard (Eds.). *Family education and early intervention* (pp. 116-126). Montreal: Editions Arc.

Tarabulsy, G.M., & Derevensky, J.L. (1990b). Coping mechanisms of elementary school children from divorced and nondivorced parents. *Canadian Psychology*, 31 (2), 298.

Tarabulsy, G.M., Kurtz, L., & Derevensky, J.L. (1991). *Coping behaviors, risk status, and children from divorced homes*. Unpublished manuscript.

Tschann, J.M., Johnston, J.R., Kline, M., & Wallerstein, J.S. (1989). Family process and children's functioning during divorce. *Journal of Marriage and the Family, 51*, 431-444.

Wallerstein, J.S., & Blakeslee, S. (1989). *Second chances. Men, women, and children a decade after divorce: Who wins, who loses–and why*. New York: Ticknor & Fields.

Wallerstein, J.S., & Kelly, J.B. (1980). *Surviving the break-up: How children actually cope with divorce*. New York: Basic Books.

Weinraub, M., Jaeger, E., & Hoffman, L.W. (1988). Predicting infant outcomes in families of employed and nonemployed mothers. *Early Childhood Research Quarterly, 3*, 361-378.

Weiss, R.S. (1979). Growing up a little faster: The experience of growing up in a single parent household. *Journal of Social Issues, 35*, 97-111.

Effects of Parental Divorce
ancial Support
lege

This page only

rissett
Furr

SUMMARY. No-fault divorce laws, and the lowering of the age of minority from 21 to 18 years have combined to have unintended negative impact on the children of divorce. Previous research has shown that children whose parents are divorced are at increased risk for emotional problems and a reduced standard of living.

This study was conducted to learn more about the effects of parental divorce on a young person's access to a college education.

A questionnaire was developed to learn how students pay for college, and what non-financial support they receive from parents. The questionnaire was administered to a randomly selected sample of 192 students at a state university.

Findings indicated that young people whose parents were divorced received higher Pell grants, were more likely to provide more of their own necessities, and were more likely to repay their college loans themselves. Further, young people whose parents were divorced were much more likely to have their material and financial needs met by their custodial parents rather than their non-custodial parents.

Barbara Grissett, PhD, is on the faculty, Department of Sociology, Social Work and Criminal Justice, ET Station, East Texas State University, Commerce, TX 75429. L. Allen Furr, PhD, is on the faculty, Department of Criminology, University of Louisville, Louisville, KY.

Address all correspondence to Professor Barbara Grissett.

[Haworth co-indexing entry note]: "Effects of Parental Divorce on Children's Financial Support for College." Grissett, Barbara, and L. Allen Furr. Co-published simultaneously in *Journal of Divorce & Remarriage* (The Haworth Press, Inc.) Vol. 22, No. 1/2, 1994, pp. 155-166; and: *The Economics of Divorce: The Effects on Parents and Children* (ed: Craig A. Everett) The Haworth Press, Inc., 1994, pp. 155-166. Multiple copies of this article/chapter may be purchased from The Haworth Document Delivery Center [1-800-3-HAWORTH; 9:00 a.m. - 5:00 p.m. (EST)].

Implications are that young people with divorced parents may have less financial support for college from their family, and the support they receive is much more likely to come from their custodial than non-custodial parent.

Changes in child support laws and financial aid policies are recommended.

Over the past five years, the literature on the effects of parental divorce has reported negative impact on children's educational attainment (Amato & Keith, 1991; Keith & Finlay, 1988; Wallerstein & Blakeslee, 1989; Fletcher, 1989; Medved, 1989). This research has focused primarily on the relationship between parents' divorce, child support, the child's school performance, and eventual educational attainment. Few studies have addressed the association between child support and other financial resources and access to college for students whose parents divorce.

In discussing possible factors that contributed to the low post-secondary attainment they found among children of divorce, Wallerstein and Blakeslee (1989) indicated that divorced mothers, who are most likely to gain legal custody of their child, were often financially unable to help with college expenses, and that child support from non-custodial fathers stopped abruptly when the child reached the age of 18. Since the law did not require support through college, many of the fathers in their study did not provide it, even though they were financially able and held college degrees themselves; indeed, a majority of their sample had graduated from college and a fourth held advanced professional degrees. Furthermore, the fathers who did help with college were more likely to help sons than daughters.

Weitzman (1985) found fewer than five percent of divorce decrees contained provisions for support of children in college. She found that mothers, who had less money than fathers, were more likely to help their children financially past the age of 18. Some of the college-age children in the study by Wallerstein and Blakeslee (1989) were going to college part-time and working, or were working full-time and trying to save for college. Some had not even attempted college though they had the aptitude to do well. Most were underachieving in their academic and career goals, yet fathers often seemed to feel exonerated by having supported their child until age 18, and believed that children should work for an education. The authors contended, however, that it was unrealistic to expect satisfactory achievement by college students who must work to support themselves as well.

The lack of court-ordered post-majority child support encouraged divorced fathers to be less honorable and less responsible in supporting their children than fathers in intact families (Weitzman, 1985). Weitzman stated that post-majority support is justified by the reality that an 18-year old is not ready for self-sufficiency in terms of expenses for education and daily living.

Because of these limitations, children of divorce often fall short of their potential in career choice and preparation. Wallerstein and Blakeslee (1985) wrote, "Divorce exerts a chilling effect on the hopes, aspirations, and achievements of our children" (p. 160). This effect is rooted in the financial insecurity that children of divorce suffer as they grow up. It is exacerbated by the diminished time and energy available to them from stressed, over-worked, financially strapped custodial parents, together with reduced emotional, physical and financial involvement of absent non-custodial parents. As children grow older, needs become more extensive and more expensive to meet. At the same time, child support does not increase, but may actually decrease or stop altogether, depending on the non-custodial parent's degree of commitment and other circumstances. Finally, just as children reach the most expensive time of dependency, that of post-secondary education, court-ordered child support obligation ends. If former non-custodial parents fail to continue voluntarily to support children during post-secondary career preparation, then children are left to rely on themselves, custodial parents (who are often drained after years of struggling financially), and whatever government aid might be available to finance college.

While qualitative studies and anecdotal evidence have indicated that this is frequently the case, no quantitative studies exploring actual sources of funding for college students from divorced families were found in the literature. The present study explored two hypotheses: (1) Children of divorced parents receive less familial financial support for college than children of intact families, and (2) When children of divorced parents receive financial help from their families, they receive it more often from their custodial parents than from their non-custodial parents.

PROCEDURES

This analysis used data collected from a random sample of students attending a medium-size, state supported university in the southwest. The sample was limited to students whose parents were most likely to cooperate in their child's education. Therefore, the sample only included students who were from 18 to 25 years of age and never married. Information was first gathered from telephone interviews. Initial review of these data indicated that students from divorced families were underrepresented. Consequently, in order to minimize sampling error among this group, a follow-up survey identified additional students whose parents were no longer married to each other. A total of 192 students were included in the analysis: 108 (56.3%) were from intact families and 84 (43.4%) from divorced ones.

Respondents were asked a series of questions that indicated the sources of their financial support while in college and the amount of that support. Children of divorced families provided specific information about the divorce such as their age at the divorce, who was awarded custody, if child support was ordered, and if the support was paid according to the conditions of the divorce settlement. In addition to descriptive statistics, log linear regression analysis was used to measure the relationships between categorical variables. In this technique, lambda coefficients and log odds are calculated. Log odds are expressed as the probability that one value or event of a categorical variable will occur as a ratio to another value or event.

FINDINGS

The data are presented in three sections: (1) primary sources of support, (2) child support, and (3) financial aid.

Primary Sources of Support. Provision of financial support for college was divided into five key areas: tuition, room and board, health care, automobile purchase and upkeep, and insurance (medical, dental, and auto). Table 1 compares primary sources of support while in college for students from intact and divorced families. All variables, with the exception of the provision and maintenance of an automobile, were related significantly to parental marital status in the hypothesized direction; that is, intact families were more likely to furnish primary support for their children in college than were divorced families. Compared with students from intact families, those with divorced parents were more likely to be financially responsible for themselves. Over half of the divorced group were accountable for their own tuition, whereas over 70 percent of the intact group's families covered these costs. In addition, intact families were more likely than divorced families to pay for room and board (75.2 percent compared to 54.4 percent) and health care (71.2 percent versus 56 percent).

Differences in insurance coverage between family types were among the more notable of these findings. As seen in Table 1, divorced parents furnished insurance at higher rates than room and board. Almost three-fourths of the divorced families provided health insurance for their child, 61 percent supplied dental insurance, and 50.7 percent carried the child's auto insurance. These rates, nevertheless, fell short of the intact families, of which 82 percent maintained medical insurance, 81.5 percent provided dental, and 52.8 percent supplied auto insurance. In comparison with students from intact families, a large number of students from divorced families reported carrying no health, dental, or auto insurance at all, a finding that suggests students from divorced families are at greater financial risk when faced with health or emotional problems or accidents.

Child Support. According to the respondents, 76.5 percent of students whose parents divorced were awarded child support from the courts; 45.3 percent of all non-custodial parents, however, either paid less than the agreed amount, failed to pay the ordered amount, or were not ordered to pay at all (Table 2). Just over half, 54.6 percent of the respondents, reported that their non-custodial parent paid child support according to the court's mandate. Though it was not the intent of this research to investigate differences in child

TABLE 1. Primary Sources of Support.

	TUITION		ROOM AND BOARD		HEALTH		CAR	
	n	%	n	%	n	%	n	%
INTACT								
Family	74	70.5	76	75.2	74	71.2	57	52.8
Self	31	29.5	25	24.8	30	28.8	39	47.2
DIVORCED								
Family	39	48.8	43	54.4	42	56.0	38	49.4
Self	41	51.3	36	45.6	33	44.0	29	37.7
Chi-Square		8.13		7.67		3.75		.27
Significance		.01		.01		.10		none

	MEDICAL		DENTAL		CAR	
	n	%	n	%	n	%
INTACT						
Family	93	86.9	88	81.5	76	73.8
Self	7	6.5	5	4.6	19	18.4
None	7	6.5	15	13.9	8	7.8
DIVORCED						
Family	60	74.1	50	61.0	38	50.7
Self	7	8.6	6	7.3	30	40.0
None	14	17.3	26	31.7	7	9.3
Chi-Square		5.97		10.14		11.07
Significance		.10		.01		.01

support awards and noncompliance in payment, we did discover that child support was awarded less frequently to children who were 15 to 18 years of age at the time their parents divorced. Courts failed to award child support to children in this age group as often as they awarded it to other age groups (log odds = 1.00). Furthermore, the compliance rate for those ordered to pay less was less than 50 percent. This finding is especially relevant as the child and the custodial parent plan for college.

Among divorced families, the economic needs of students were not equally shared between custodial and non-custodial parents. Table 3 indicates that custodial parents and the students themselves

TABLE 2. Child's Age at Divorce and Support Adequacy.

	CHILD SUPPORT*					
	Yes		No		Lambda	Log
AGE AT DIVORCE	n	%	n	%	Coef.	Odds
0 to 5	23	82.1	5	17.9	.186	4.27
6 to 10	18	75.0	6	25.0	–.017	2.85
11 to 14	15	88.2	2	11.8	.371	6.20
15 to 18	6	50.0	6	50.0	–.540	1.00
Column Total	62	76.5	19	23.5		

* Significant at .10, chi-square = 6.48

	SUPPORT COMPLIANCE**					
	Yes		No		Lambda	Log
AGE AT DIVORCE	n	%	n	%	Coef.	Odds
0 to 5	14	51.9	13	48.1	–.0758	1.07
6 to 10	12	52.2	11	47.8	–.0698	1.09
11 to 14	11	68.8	5	14.7	.2572	2.09
15 to 18	5	44.4	5	55.6	–.1115	1.00
Column Total	41	54.6	34	45.3		

**No significant difference

bore the greatest financial burden of attending college. On all variables, custodial parents were at least twice as likely to provide support as non-custodial parents. At one extreme, custodial parents were six times more likely than non-custodial parents to provide room and board for their child in college. The smallest difference between the two parents was found in tuition support and provision of an automobile, but for both of these categories, the student was more likely to pay than either parent. Non-custodial parents, in fact, contributed more than the student on only two variables: medical and dental insurance. Note again that the percentage of students without medical insurance was the same as the number whose non-custodial parent provided it, and that more students lived without dental insurance than those whose non-custodial parent provided this coverage. In summary, non-custodial parents contributed far less to the financial needs of their children in college than either custodial parents or their children.

TABLE 3. Differences in Support Within Divorced Families.

	Custodial Parent		Non-Cust.		Step-Parent		Self		Other		None	
	n	%	n	%	n	%	n	%	n	%	n	%
Tuition	24	30.0	10	12.5	1	1.3	41	51.3	4	5.0		na
Board	36	43.4	6	7.2	1	1.2	36	43.4	4	4.8		na
Health	30	39.0	11	14.3	1	1.3	33	42.9	2	2.6		na
Auto	24	29.3	11	13.4	3	3.7	29	35.4	5	6.1	10	12.2
Insurance												
Medical	43	52.4	14	17.1	3	3.7	7	8.5	1	1.2	14	17.1
Dental	35	42.2	11	13.3	4	4.8	6	7.2	1	1.2	26	31.3
Auto	31	40.3	6	7.8	1	1.3	30	39.0	2	2.6	7	9.1

Totals sum to over 100 percent due to rounding

Institutional Financial Aid. Not surprisingly, students from divorced families procured guaranteed student loans and Pell grants more than students from intact families (Table 4). One-third of students from divorced families received loans to pay for college, while about 22 percent of intact families' students borrowed money. Though the amount of student loans did not differ by family type, the plans for repayment varied significantly. Of respondents from intact families, 62.5 percent were responsible for repaying their loans, while 96.2 percent of students from divorced families were similarly responsible. Only one of the 27 students from divorced families who received loans indicated the family would be responsible for repaying the loan.

Pell grants, federal education grants awarded by need, were distributed unequally as well. About 40 percent of students from divorced families received grants compared to only 19 percent of those from intact families. Furthermore, students from divorced families received larger Pell grant awards than students from intact families. This indicates that students from divorced families in this sample could demonstrate greater financial need and fewer resources than students from intact families.

DISCUSSION

The purpose of this study was to examine the effects of parental divorce on financial resources available to college students. The

TABLE 4. Institutional Support

	INTACT		DIVORCED	
	n	%	n	%
STUDENT LOANS				
Yes	23	21.5	28	33.7
No	84	78.5	55	66.3
Total	107	56.3	83	43.7
Chi-Square = 2.97				
Significance = .10				
PELL GRANTS				
Yes	20	18.9	33	39.3
No	86	81.1	51	60.7
Total	106	55.8	84	44.2
Chi-Square = 28.09				
Significance = .005				
REPAYING LOANS				
Self	15	62.5	26	92.5
Family	9	37.5	1	3.6
Total	24	46.2	27	53.8
Chi-Square = 10.1				
Significance = .01				
LOAN AMOUNTS				
Mean	$1,779		$1,406	
St. Dev.	$1,855		$1,129	
F-Score = 1.55				
No significance				
PELL AMOUNTS				
Mean	$1,342		$1,787	
St. Dev.	$ 735		$1,185	
F-Score = 2.60				
Significance = .05				

data revealed that college students with divorced parents received less financial support from their families than did students whose parents were still married. This was the case, not only in an overall sense, but also in each of the important categories studied. Further, students from divorced families relied much more on their custodial parents, themselves, and government aid than on their non-custodial parents to meet financial needs.

Students with divorced parents received significantly more financial aid from Pell grants, indicating lower financial resources in their custodial parents' households than in the households of students from intact families. This finding is consistent with the literature reporting that the inadequacies of court-ordered child support, together with poor compliance with the orders, contribute to increased financial hardships for children of divorce and their custodial parents (Fletcher, 1989; Nicholas-Casebolt & Danziger, 1989; Weitzman, 1985; Williams, 1986). There is clearly a need for changes in child support laws and financial aid policies, and for future research into this effect of divorce.

The United States does not provide post-secondary education free of charge to young people. The system assumes that families of young people will provide them with appropriate career preparation. The findings of this study suggest that children from divorced families did not in fact receive adequate parental support as often as did their peers from intact families.

Federal and state governments and many institutions of higher learning provide partial assistance with college costs when a family demonstrates financial hardship. The practice of examining the resources available to a student in determining eligibility for financial aid includes a complete review of the financial situation of the student's parents, including assets, liabilities, and income. The student is also asked to report income from other sources, such as scholarships, wages, interest, and financial help from others. When a student's parents are divorced, financial information must be provided for the parent with whom the student lived the most during the past year, or the parent who supported the student the most. Usually, this is the custodial parent. If that parent is remarried, the step-parent's resources are also reported. If the student receives any assistance from the other parent, that is reported as "other income" to the student.

Financial aid offices determine a student's total costs to attend college and then specify, based on the family's and student's resources, what the student's and family's contribution should be. Pell grants and student loans are then offered to help overcome any deficit. For a student with divorced parents, the implication is clear: The custodial parent is expected to contribute a certain amount as is the student, and the financial aid package will provide for some or all of the balance of the student's needs. There is no expectation placed upon the non-custodial parent. Again, the message is unmistakable: The non-custodial parent is no longer considered responsible, yet the custodial parent is. In addition, a step-parent's resources are assumed to be available to the student. If not holding the non-custodial parent responsible is based on child support ending at age 18, then upon what basis does financial aid policy require a student to furnish financial information on either parent? If non-custodial parents are no longer financially responsible when their child turns 18, then is it equitable that parents who have never divorced and custodial parents are still held responsible? The most pragmatic way to restore equality would be to affirm through policy that all parents are responsible to support their children until the end of dependency, i.e., until the child is prepared to begin appropriate employment. This policy change alone would be inadequate to insure coverage of financial needs for children of divorced parents. In fact, in states where child support ends when a child is 18 and financial aid offices consider the resources of a non-custodial parent who does not contribute to college expenses, governmental aid may be denied, thus effectively blocking the student from college (Wallerstein & Blakeslee, 1989). In order to prevent this, legislatures should amend child support laws to require continued support until the child completes post-secondary education. The determination of what is appropriate for each child should be made at the time of the divorce, based on the parents' resources, and the interests and aptitude of the child. Like other features of divorce decrees, such provisions could be amended if warranted by future circumstances.

Further research is needed to learn more about how and why divorce impacts children's educational attainment. Research is especially needed to: (1) examine how the socioeconomic and educational level of divorced parents affect their support of college age children; (2) determine which divorce-related factors may increase risk of parental non-support for children's college; (3) evaluate the effectiveness of court-ordered college support where this is required by law, as well as when it is done voluntarily; and (4) learn the distribution of children of divorce in various post-secondary educational settings, including vocational and trade schools, junior colleges, and private, small public, and large public senior colleges.

In summary, the results of this study show that a negative, though unintended, effect of divorce is reduced financial access to a college education for children of divorce. If future research substantiates this finding, major changes in child support law and financial aid policy are indicated.

REFERENCES

Amato, P.R., & Keith, B. (1991). Parental Divorce and Adult Well-Being: A Meta-Analysis. *Journal of Marriage and the Family*, 53(1), 43-58.

Fletcher, C.N. (1989). A comparison of Incomes and Expenditures of Male-Headed Households Paying Child Support and Female-Headed Households Receiving Child Support, *Family Relations*, 38, 412-417.

Gabardi, L., & Rosen, L.A. (1991). Differences Between College Students from Divorced and Intact Families. *Journal of Divorce & Remarriage*, 15(3/4), 175-191.

Keith, V.M., & Finlay, B. (1988). The Impact of Parental Divorce on Children's Educational Attainment, Marital Timing, and Likelihood of Divorce. *Journal of Marriage and the Family*, 50, 797-809.

Medved, D. (1989). *The Case Against Divorce*. New York: Ivy.

Nichols-Casebolt, A., & Dahziger, S.K. (1989). The Effect of Childbearing Age on Child Support Awards and Economic Well-Being Among Divorcing Mothers. *Journal of Divorce*, 12 (4), 35-48.

Seltzer, J.A., Schaeffer, N.C., & Charng, H. (1989). Family Ties After Divorce: The Relationships between Visiting and Paying Child Support. *Journal of Marriage and the Family*, 51, 1014-1032.

Wallerstein, J.S., & Blakeslee, S. (1989). *Second Chances: Men, Women, and Children a Decade After Divorce*. New York: Ticknor and Fields.

Wallerstein, J.S., & Kelly, J.B. (1980). *Surviving the Breakup: How Children and Parents Cope with Divorce*. New York: Ticknor and Fields.

Weitzman, L.J. (1985). *The Divorce Revolution: The Unexpected Social and Economic Consequences for Women and Children in America*. New York: The Free Press.

Williams, R.G. (1986). The Analyst's Corner: The Inadequacy of Child Support Orders; Implications for Policy Development. *New England Journal of Human Services*, 6(3), 34-36.

For Product Safety Concerns and Information please contact our EU representative GPSR@taylorandfrancis.com Taylor & Francis Verlag GmbH, Kaufingerstraße 24, 80331 München, Germany

Batch number: 10725979

Printed by Printforce, the Netherlands